Essential Software *Testing*

A Use-Case Approach

GREG FOURNIER

CRC Press
Taylor & Francis Group
Boca Raton London New York

CRC Press is an imprint of the
Taylor & Francis Group, an **informa** business
AN AUERBACH BOOK

Essential Software *Testing*

A Use-Case Approach

CRC Press
Taylor & Francis Group
6000 Broken Sound Parkway NW, Suite 300
Boca Raton, FL 33487-2742

ISBN 13: 978-1-138-44048-7 (hbk)
ISBN 13: 978-1-4200-8981-3 (pbk)

Visit the Taylor & Francis Web site at
http://www.taylorandfrancis.com

and the Auerbach Web site at
http://www.auerbach-publications.com

TABLE OF CONTENTS

DEDICATION

This book is dedicated to the memory of my father, Lionel, who I think about every day.

PREFACE

Let's face it.

The formal part of software testing is a bore and a necessary evil at best.

At least that is what most people in software development will tell you. Testers are on projects to point out mistakes. Who wants to do that?

Well that *is* a perception, and this book isn't going to change it.

What this book *will* do is skip the ceremony and present testing concepts, tying them together in a sequential and straightforward fashion. At the same time, war stories will be interjected to spice things up a bit. The book will describe testing methods and techniques in a common sense manner that is easy to understand.

I want to communicate how to determine what to test and how to test it, how to select proper tests to match the plan, techniques to build and trace tests, and finally how to conduct and record tests.

I know, this all sounds simple, but things get convoluted in the testing world.

So, before I get into some of the cool details of the book and who it is written for, let's talk about what you won't find in it.

First, you won't find much talk about how important testing is. You already know that. I don't want to waste your time spewing a bunch of hot air about how smart it is to test. I would rather talk about when it is important to test.

I won't spend time talking about how hard testing can be. Instead I'll show ways to make it simple.

Finally, this book won't dig too deep into implementation specific testing. There is plenty of material out there that explains OO testing techniques, embedded software testing, tool use, etc.

Instead, I'll get you to the point where you can implement your project specific testing solution. I'll focus on:

– fitting testing activities into any process. This isn't a one size fits all thing. Warning – there's some thinking involved!

– testing in an agile manner rather than testing within an agile process - a big difference. The agile word is overused, but I'm going to use it to mean being as lean and mean as a given project and environment will allow.

– important testing concepts to lay the groundwork for the rest of the book.

– test planning and a simple test process that can be adjusted to fit most projects.

– specific techniques to handle the pieces of the process including understanding requirements, identifying potential tests, selecting and building tests, tracing artifacts, and executing tests.

– pulling everything together with a real world example.

Why this book is important

I've gotten sick and tired of hearing how hard testing is and how careful one has to be. There's a lot written on testing, but you have to really dig for practical help.

I haven't read anything that hits on the important activities in a clear and concise manner. This book attempts to fill that void.

Who this book is for

This book is for anyone who wants to understand how to test efficiently and actively enhance overall project quality. It is also for anyone who wants to get a handle on Use Case driven testing techniques.

Software development managers and project managers can use the book to become familiar with incorporating test processes into larger project processes. This book describes a proactive approach to testing with supporting frameworks that managers and testing personnel will be able to use. Managers can use the concepts and techniques described here to aid in project and test planning and in the training of test personnel. Test people can use the book as a step-by-step guide to perform testing activities in a manner that helps the entire project.

How to use this book

Use it in any manner you see fit.

There are three parts to this book. You can read those parts in the order you want. If you are more interested in testing activities and techniques, jump to part two or three. No matter what order you read the book in, read it all. There is too much good stuff you won't want to miss.

Part One talks about making testing agile. If you are trying to get insight into how testing can be done efficiently in different process environments take a look at this section.

Part Two lays the foundation for the rest of the book by describing testing concepts. Skim through this section if you have been around testing for a while and are already familiar with the concepts described.

Part Three shows how to test. It details specific testing activities that can be used on almost any project. Specifically, Use Case driven testing is described. I will show you how to test using Use Cases regardless of what the official requirements of your project are. Use this part of the book as a testing guide.

ACKNOWLEDGMENTS

Without the help and support of the following people, this book would have never become a reality. So…

I want to thank the folks at IconATG including Beth, Stella, and Lou. I have been associated with them for many years and because of them had the opportunity to work on many fun projects.

Thanks to Stephanie Stone also of IconATG who provided valuable feedback related to software requirements.

I want to thank Mike Henry for some great pictures he provided for the cover and interior.

Thanks to Andrea Waugh, my daughter, who happens to be a Project Manager. She spent time reviewing this book for me. Her insight and down to earth perspective definitely made this book better.

Thanks to my good friend David DeWitt for the time and effort he spent supplying feedback and insight. There is no reason to write a book if there isn't a good idea and a need. David shed light on the need for this book and helped cultivate the idea. We worked together on a number of projects where we developed many of the techniques described in this book. He provided me with a sandbox to play in among other things. David shows up in some of the war stories in this book, always as a one of the good guys.

Thanks to Paul Evitts, my friend, writing mentor, and editor. It would be an understatement to say this book wouldn't be possible without him. He's been through this process before with his own book and walked me through each step of the way. When I discussed some of the cool things I had been doing, he encouraged me to write a book about them. He told me that if I wrote the book he would edit it. He didn't know what he was getting himself into. Paul is an excellent writer and coached me into becoming a better writer as the book progressed. He spent many hours editing this book and making sure concepts and techniques were clearly explained while still exuding my enthusiasm and passion I have for the topic. Thanks to him, I can now spel.

Thanks to my mother Betty who with my father, led by example to instill a strong work ethic in me and my siblings. I also want to thank my son Jeff, and my grandchildren Alan and Maya, who have all enriched my life.

And last, but not least, I extend my most heartfelt gratitude and ever lasting love to my wife, Jen, who understands me deeply and supports me completely. Without her I wouldn't have been able to accomplish half of what I have, let alone the writing of this book. She supported the idea from the start and helped keep me motivated through the entire process. She also provided valuable input into the design of the cover and picture selection.

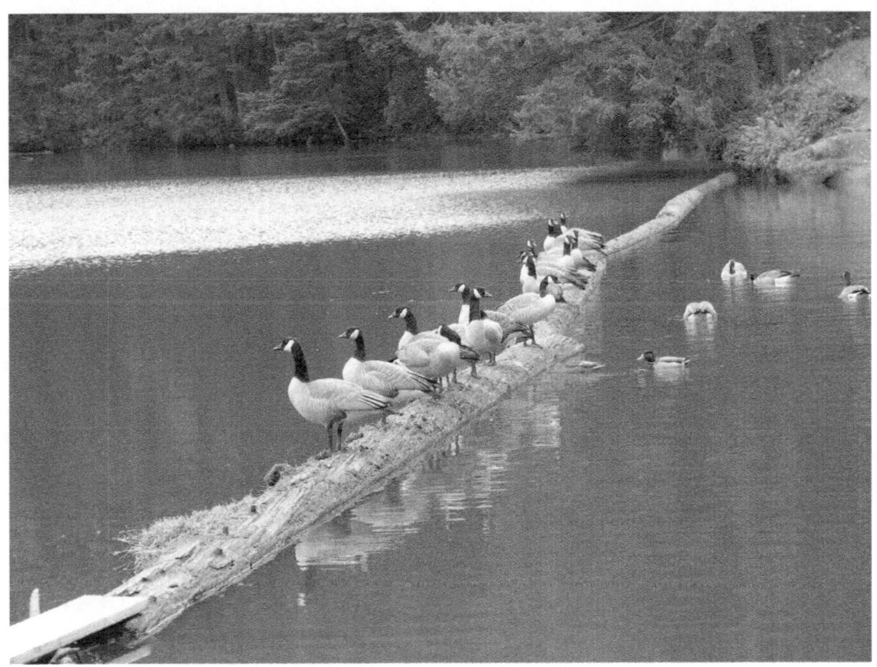

Part One

Testing Essentially

This section will help you understand what it really means to be agile in testing. In this part of the book, I first discuss basic testing concepts and examples to get things started. I then cover bringing agility into testing or as I call it, Essential Testing. This will set the stage for the rest of the book.

I'll cover

- Basic testing concepts
- Examples that will be referenced throughout the book
- The concept of Essential Testing
- The difference between being agile in testing and testing on projects using an Agile methodology
- How to be agile on any project regardless of methodology

Chapter 1

On Being A Tester

The first time I worked as a tester on a project, I met with a developer to informally review his first deliverable, part of a customer service system.

I was the testing lead and it was my idea to conduct early informal reviews, figuring a little initial interaction with other teams on the project would help improve quality. The developer was a friend of mine and we had worked on many other projects together in various roles.

As I entered my friend's cube, he handed me a pair of pliers.

"What're these for?" I asked. He replied "Now that you're one of 'them' you'll eventually pull my finger nails out." He figured we might as well get started then and there.

I was taken aback a bit, but not surprised. I knew what he was talking about and often had similar feelings about testers.

Usually, project team members think of testers like this:

- Testers are rigid.
- Testers are anal, more concerned about pointing out failures than about the big picture.
- Testers wait until the last minute to discover problems, causing project delays and making the project team look bad.

- Then they gloat.

Okay, this is a little extreme.... but not far off the mark.

Testing Perceptions and Realities

Perceptions

On most projects testing is considered a necessary evil similar to *(aargh)* Configuration Management. Testing helps the project, but it's hard to imagine what type of person would want to do that type of job full time.

Of course, testers frequently see project realities differently, and react to circumstances in a way that reinforces stereotypes.

For example, testers are often left out of the early stages of projects when requirements are being developed, but are expected to write tests against requirements that are not always testable and often ambiguous. Then code gets thrown over the wall to be tested towards the end of the development process or iteration – usually late - with builds often dead on arrival. This causes a bottleneck in testing, which makes the testing team look bad.

So testers, knowing what is in store for them, take appropriate CYA measures. Many of these measures make good sense given the circumstances, however they may be perceived by the development team and management.

This includes exhaustive testing (*perceived* as being anal), detailed bug reports (*perceived* as finger pointing), and detailed progress reporting (*perceived* as gloating), all of which are perceived as evidence of testers being rigid.

Reality

The reality? Many testers, given the opportunity, prefer working on projects using a more agile development process, one where the emphasis is placed on test driven development.

Developers write tests before they write code and have the luxury of having direct access to the people who will eventually accept the product.... and less time is spent worrying about DOA builds and products that don't come close to meeting stakeholder expectations.

But, testers usually don't have the opportunity to choose the types of projects they work on. And most projects employ processes where the place and time for testing is usually towards the end of a project, phase, or iteration.

And then there are the usual development dysfunctions - for example, around requirements. Sometimes requirements aren't great, other times they may not exist. I have worked on projects where development was started before formal requirements were even written, but we were expected to test against the requirements.

Another testing approach to deal with reality

In this book, I will be introducing the concept I call Essential Testing... tools for testers. This is not really a new concept, but an approach to testing that works with both of the usual approaches to development these days: Agile Development or development using some variation of the Unified Process. It also works with all the legacy and mongrel processes that are probably even more typical of system development these days. And it provides an additional benefit, an awareness of that new 21st century need – governance.

Essential Testing says test the right things to the right level of detail at the right time, providing results in the proper context to prove the system under test with the most efficient amount of effort. It sounds straight-forward, but getting it right requires a great deal of proactive-ness on the part of the testing organization, and a great deal of cooperation by all project team members.

Testing In an Agile Way.... But Not Agile Testing

In Essential Testing it's up to testing professionals to take the bull by the horns in an effort to change their situation. By taking a different approach to testing, testers *can* be proactive, and agile.

Being Agile and Proactive

True agility is where you make an effort to understand the entire project environment up front, understand the perception of a successful system, and take actions early to help everyone succeed.

As a tester, being proactive and agile means knowing the environment you are testing in, knowing who it is you need to prove the system either works or doesn't, understanding what needs to be presented to prove the system, taking action early to ensure success, knowing you are going to make mistakes, and being willing to adapt.

For testing, this may mean taking matters in your own hands - without being intrusive - and helping perform tasks that are not usually associated with testing. All of which takes skills not usually associated with testing:

- Communication becomes important to understand the project environment and help mold it early.
- Boldness is also needed to be able to have confidence in the actions taken and the ability to adapt when things need to be changed.
- And, of course, agility. I'll cover agility in detail in a later chapter, including what people think it is and how testers can truly be agile.

Dealing With Governance

These days, testers have to think "governance". This affects not just projects in industries where the government has a responsibility for public interest (like flight systems, health regulation, or financial reporting), but increasingly within industries - self governance.

Governance concerns can add layers of bureaucracy and whole new stakeholders who must be satisfied that the product(s) being developed meets their expectations. Many products, such as ones dealing with flight over civilian airspace, or products used in health care, must be certified before they can be used.

Testers can also be proactive in environments where there is a high level of governance. It still comes down to knowing the environment and the expectations of the stakeholders. In the chapters to follow we will deal with Essential Testing in all environments including those where governance is a major issue.

War Story

I once was tasked with creating a requirements elicitation and management process for an organization. I worked with the team responsible for requirements and part of our goal was to deploy a requirements management tool to augment the process.

We would eventually present our findings to the manager who would ultimately own the process. I was told this wouldn't be an easy task since the manager came from a testing background and had a tendency to be "detail oriented".

I thought having a tester in charge of requirements elicitation and management was a great idea. Who better to understand the steps needed to ensure good requirements than someone who has dealt with them from a testing perspective?

I was half right.

When we presented our plan to the manager it was clear she understood the processes required to ensure good

continued...

requirements - she was all for the processes, controls and tools proposed to help ensure requirements were well written and stable requirements.

But, she was more focused on the reporting aspects of the tool.

In particular, she wanted to be able to report on inadequate and rapidly changing requirements. I assured her that while we could produce those types of reports, with the proper processes and controls in place, they would be less important. This was difficult for her to grasp, because as a tester, she usually dealt with inadequate and changing requirements rather than ensuring requirements are right to begin with.

As testers we may know what good artifacts and processes are, but we also need to be able to understand the best use of our time to get things right. This will be vital as we cover ways of taking new approaches to testing.

CHAPTER 2

Basic Concepts Boot Camp

Before we get into the details of how to do Essential Testing and how it may be different from the testing your father did, I need to make sure The Reader is up to speed on some basic concepts that are the groundwork for all the later discussions. Except for 'The Real Basics', everything here will be covered in much greater detail as the book unfolds.

The Real Basics

Black Box Testing

Black box testing refers to testing a software item without knowing anything about its inner workings - about how it does the job! The system under test is actually treated as a black box. Tests are written to specifications describing what the software should do, based on specified inputs and expected outputs.

This is real requirements based testing - a tester and programmer can work independently of each other from the same set of requirements as soon as requirements are delivered. Black box tests can be created to test a product independently of the individuals responsible for its development. The tester doesn't need to have knowledge of the implementation and can create tests based on requirements. This form of testing can also help identify holes in requirements.

White Box Testing

White box testing focuses on the internal structure of the system under test. Paths through the software are identified and tested. This requires knowledge of the programming language being used. For systems that come under high governance, such as software certified by the FAA, white box testing can be used to supplement black box testing to ensure all code paths are covered.

Unit Testing

This is a particular kind of white box testing. Properly done, it ensures all paths through the test object are executed.

Unit testing is conducted on individual modules of source code. Developers perform unit tests to ensure the component they build works. What constitutes a unit depends on what is being built and the methodology used. For example, in Object Oriented development a Class could be considered the smallest unit to test.

As units are integrated into components and products we get the real picture of whether the unit works. Unit testing is usually the job of the developer - and, being agile, we won't concern ourselves with the developer's job.

Functional Requirements

These describe a system's externally-perceived functionality from the viewpoint of a stakeholder/user. The system is treated as a black box.

Non-Functional Requirements

These are conditions the system must satisfy that go beyond the functionality of the system. They usually cover things the system must do along with the things described in the functional requirements. Categories of non-functional requirements include:

- System Wide Capabilities such as security, auditing, and error handling
- Safety
- Reliability and Availability
- Performance
- Usability
- Software Design Goals
- Design and Development Constraints

Non-functional requirements tend to be a mix of requirements that describe what the system does, and how it does them. Consider performance requirements, they will describe what the system must accomplish in terms of response time. Other performance related requirements could describe how response times are actually met by the system, including solutions such as load balancing.

Stakeholder Needs

These are the needs of the people for whom the system is being built. The needs are described in non-system terms. They can be evaluated and turned into something the system can satisfy. In the case of a website for a hockey league described in the next chapter, a stakeholder need would be "The website sponsor needs to be able to provide search services to hockey players who wish to find places to play hockey". Another is "The website sponsor needs to be able to provide team management services to team managers". These are general statements of needs that can be satisfied by multiple means.

Features

These could be considered the highest level of system requirements. These are usually derived from stakeholder needs and describe software features that will produce benefit to stakeholders. In the case of the hockey site, features could include "the ability of the system to provide capability to search for hockey venues" and "team management capabilities".

Testing Concepts

Traceability

Traceability in software development and testing refers to cross referencing requirements, for example tracing from requirements to supporting tests. The level of traceability varies from project to project depending on the need to show relationships between artifacts.

On one extreme, projects do no traceability. The other extreme..., full traceability: requirements may trace up to features and down to design artifacts, source code, and tests, i.e. Tests trace to requirements, design, and code.

While traceability is a good thing from a verification and project management perspective, it can be difficult to manage on a large scale. As changes occur, links between artifacts may be broken and require change management.

Coverage

I talk about two levels of coverage in this book.

The first is requirements coverage by tests: are there sufficient tests to cover requirements to the level of detail needed so the system can be considered proven?

The other is code coverage: is the source code covered by tests?

There are a number of different ways of measuring code coverage such as:

- Statement Coverage - Has each line of the source code been executed and tested?

- Condition Coverage - Has each evaluation point (such as a true/false decision) been executed and tested for all possible conditions?
- Path Coverage - Has every possible route through a given part of the code been executed and tested?
- Entry/Exit Coverage - Has every possible call and return of the function been executed and tested?
- Decision Coverage – Has every possible condition been tested to show that it can independently alter the condition?

Note: safety critical applications are often required to demonstrate that testing achieves 100% of some form of code coverage.

There are tools that measure code coverage. They detect level of coverage as each test is run. But, while tools help, they may not be enough - code inspections may be necessary.

Varieties of Essential Requirements

Traditional Requirements

For this book, traditional requirements are defined as requirements that take the form of "The system shall…" statements. These can vary in granularity, but should describe the complete behavior of a system.

Traditional requirements have been around for a long time.

The expectation, more from developers and the clients they seduce, is that requirements are understandable, to a level of detail that tests can be written against them and software design and development activities can take place to satisfy them.

There are usually lots of requirements that specify what

the system does, or shall do. These are also called static requirements: each requirement isolates a thing the system must do.

The problem with static requirements is that they don't always provide a clear understanding of how requirements interact, or the sequence in which the actions described by the requirements should be executed.

We tend to look at traditional requirements individually. This can lead to testing requirements that work, but don't work together. Often the requirements are grouped by functionality, but it is usually up to the user of the requirements to understand the requirements in the proper context.

From a testing perspective, the requirements may be crystal clear, but testing them can be difficult.

A very large number of projects use traditional requirements, and although they can potentially cause confusion, there are things that that can be done to help keep them clear. This is where Use Cases come in.

Use Cases

If somebody put a gun to my head and told me I could only chose one artifact for use on a project, my choice would be Use Cases. While there are some other artifacts almost as useful, without Use Cases those artifacts are much more difficult to use.

Many people have an idea of what Use Cases are. I'll start by defining them as scenarios expressing requirements based on the perspective of users of the system.

Use Cases are used to package, at a minimum, the functional requirements of a system. They are described via sequences of interaction between one or more *Actors*, who represent users, or other systems that interact with the system, and the System being specified.

Each Use Case specifies a use of the system, usually in achieving a business goal, a use that provides measurable value for the Actor.

Use Case *Specifications* are written using language that should be understandable by all associated with the system – especially including end users and analysts - avoiding technical language. They are often coauthored by business analysts and end users. They should not be confused with Use Case diagrams that use UML notation to depict Use Cases and relationships to Actors, but don't go into the detail of what a Use Case does.

The level of detail and formality written into a Use Case depends on the audience and the needs of the project employing them. A typical outline of a formal Use Case Specification may include the following:

- Use Case Name
- Summary
- Preconditions
- Basic flow of events
- Alternate flows
- Post conditions
- Business Rules
- Associated Use Cases
- Notes & Assumptions

User Stories

User Stories are requirements that take the form of about three sentences written in the language of users of the system. These have their roots in Extreme Programming, but are now used in many agile processes. They can be considered informal from a traditional perspective – and even by Unified Process types. User stories are a quick way of handling customer requirements without having to deal with large formal requirement documents and tedious tasks related to maintaining them.[1]

Safety Critical Requirements

Since this book will discuss testing safety critical applications as well, here are some critical notions to remember.

High Level Requirements

The requirements for the system in the traditional sense, created to meet the standards of 'quality requirements', that is, they meet industry standards for quality including clarity, consistency, and un-ambiguity. Quality, or what makes up good requirements, will be covered in greater detail in Ch 8.

High level requirements describe the system in terms of "what" it is supposed to do, including both functional and non-functional requirements. They are produced through analysis of system functionality and constraints, and to some degree the system architecture. These are created to meet the standards of good requirements early in a project and are used in the design and implementation of the system. High-level requirements are verified as part of acceptance testing.

These requirements, based on system functionality, are called high level because they may be further decomposed into low level requirements that can be represented by the system design. Typically, black box testing is conducted against these high level requirements.

Low Level Requirements

Low level requirements are software requirements from which source code can be directly implemented without further information. They describe "how" the system is to be implemented. These are "design requirements". (Note:

---

1 http://en.wikipedia.org/wiki/User_story

If source code can be directly implemented from high-level requirements, then those requirements will also be labeled as low level.) Airborne Systems are a case in point. For these, normal requirements are called *high level requirements*, and they are supplemented by 'design level' requirements called *low level requirements*.

In most projects, the end user cares less about how or why the system does its job as long as it does it correctly. But, in some projects, this isn't good enough - especially with safety critical systems where the stakeholder wants to be sure the design isn't sacrificing critical safety.

Low level requirements need to be formally identified when it is important ensure that the design is implemented properly.

Derived Requirements

Often during development, a specific need or implementation doesn't align with the high or low level requirements under consideration. Some may consider this a "discovered" requirement. For safety critical systems these are called derived requirements and must be reported to a safety hazard assessment team. An example is a circumstance where a system reset is required should an error occur. The safety hazard assessment team would have to approve a derived requirement for unexpected system reset.

Organizing Your Testing

Test Plans

These are documents that spell out how you will test in order to prove the system and what activities will be followed to get the job done. These plans can vary in level of formality and detail. We will get into planning the test in detail later in the book with the focus on planning just enough.

Test plans should be no more detailed than they have to be

with a focus on less. All details don't have to be known either. Every project I have been on where we had an elaborate Test Plan, we wound up changing it considerably. We need them; we just don't need to put too much faith in them.

Test Cases

A common definition of a Test Case is a description of conditions and expected results that taken together fully test a requirement or Use Case. In this book I allow multiple requirements to be described in a single Test Case and may limit a Test Case to a portion of a Use Case such as a flow of events. Written Test Cases should include a description of the functionality to be tested, and the preparation required to ensure that the test can be conducted.

Test Procedures

Test Procedures describe specific activities taken by a tester to set up, execute, and analyze a test. This includes defining data values, input and output files, automated tests to run, and detailed manual test activities.

The purpose of this artifact is to guide the tester in executing multiple tests, including:

- how to set up the test environment
- where to find test data sets
- where to put them
- the steps to execute the tests, and
- what to do with the test results.

Test Procedures can be written for manual tests, automated tests, or a combination of the two. They are usually only needed if testing is complex.

Test Scripts

A tests script is what is used to test the functionality of a software system. These scripts can be either manual or automated.

Manual test scripts are usually written scripts that the tester must perform. This implies direct interaction between the tester and the system under tests. Manual test scripts specify step-by-step instructions of what the tester should enter into the system and expected results. Many times the scripts are embedded into the Test Procedures.

Automated test scripts are software programs written to test the system. These can be generated with tools or coded the old fashioned way. Usually there is a scripting language involved to control performing the tests in an orderly manner. These tests are usually initiated by testers and are referenced in Test Procedures.

CHAPTER 3

Examples From My Experience We'll Work With

Here are three examples of projects I have done. The names have been changed to protect the innocent. I will draw on these throughout the book. Each example demonstrates different expectations and consequently, different levels of software testing rigor.

Experience 1: Rinkratz

RinkRatz is an example of working with stakeholders who are more focused on getting an end-product out the door than they are on the details of testing. They want something that works, and assume that the development team is composed of professionals who can deliver.

The product is a hockey website geared toward adult hockey players. The project is funded by a hockey nut, Denny Lemieux, who wants to make adult hockey more accessible and hopefully make a buck or two at the same time. He is the primary stakeholder and ultimate customer.

Denny is keen on an agile approach (he has programmer friends) and wants to work closely with the development team. His expectations: he just wants the site to look nice and have the functionality work with no major known defects.

One of the key features he wants is being able to search for venues to play all types of hockey: pick up games, leagues, and tournaments. As a business guy, he travels a lot, loves to be able to look for chances to play when he's on the road, but he's also the manager (and sponsor!!) of a local team.

So, naturally, another feature he wants is the ability to manage teams and leagues. He figures this feature should be offered for a small fee, but plans to let his buddies try out the features for a season to work out the bugs before selling it.

The Testing Perspective

In the above scenario the testers only have to satisfy Denny Lemieux. Functional testing can be fairly informal for the most part. The stakeholder will get a clear understanding of system capabilities as they are developed. Requirements will initially be the scenarios that have been developed. These may be supplemented by user stories. As the project progresses, if more formality is required - Denny may need outside funding and another stakeholder comes into the picture - Use Cases can be developed and Use Case based testing can be performed as required.

Experience 2: The Conveyor System Project

The Conveyor System project is an example of working with customers who are used to seeing things work in a physical environment while ensuring that the software is consistent with architectural needs.

The major stakeholder, Jimmy Bland, is the Senior Vice President in charge of Conveyor System product development. The end product to him is a system that consists of both hardware and software. He spent most of his life as an electrical engineer and is less concerned with the software aspects of the system than seeing boxes go around a conveyor system as fast as the laws of physics allow.

In this case it will be important to prove the software meets functional specifications, but also meets architectural needs as well. For this situation the underlying architecture must be proven to work with various hardware types.

Top Notch Engineering is an engineering company that has been a major player in the Conveyor System industry for over 30 years. The company has a majority market share due to big contracts with most large retail companies that have large distribution centers. Top Notch's largest selling conveyor system is 15 years old. The conveyor system is a combination of conveyor hardware with a dedicated PC card that holds software that controls system operation. There is also a PC attached that is used by end users to monitor and interact with the system.

While it is a reliable product, Top Notch's competitors are developing products that leverage the many technological changes that have happened in the last 15 years. Top Notch has only been able to keep its market share based on customer loyalty and product dependability. But with new competitive products emerging, Top Notch has been hard at work.

The software to support the current conveyor system is process oriented and considered brittle. For each installation of a conveyor system, the software must be modified to support the specific hardware configuration (distances between photo eyes, length of belts, locations of scanners, etc.). It also only accommodates a specific set of hardware components. Additions of new types of conveyor components will require major revisions or rewrites of the software application.

Top Notch has decided to add new conveyor components to its product line through a combination of internal R&D and acquisitions of smaller companies that have created such products.

Their goal is to create a product line that combines existing conveyor components along with the newly developed and acquired conveyor components. New conveyor systems would be composed of a combination of new and legacy sub-systems. Current conveyor systems would be upgraded where necessary to fit the customer's needs.

Top Notch's system software is unable to support this new direction. It will have to be rewritten. The software must support both the conveyor systems in the field and new systems that will be a combination of major sub-systems.

Top Notch IT management feels that an object-oriented approach would be the best solution - based on professed advantages of reuse. The development team is using the Unified Process (UP) for its process, so testing will have to fit into this process.

And then there are some serious technical constraints that needed to be managed. While these would typically be spelled out very clearly in the specifications, they also need to be taken into account by the test team.

The constraints derive from the need to handle 'legacy' customers, the backbone of Top Notch's success. For example:

Even though faster processors become available, existing systems will not be upgraded when the new software is installed. The new software must work on last generation processors. (a technical description of the product can be found in Appendix A).

Additionally, the system has other constraints:

- Must be configurable – changes to existing software should not be required for each installation of a conveyor system.
- Real-time performance is an issue – there is a 200 millisecond window in which all external signals must

be registered based on the speed requirements of the conveyor belts.

- Incorporation of sub-systems must be transparent – some of the sub-systems will have their own management software that must communicate with the core controlling application while other components will rely on the core application. Each sub-system should be easily configurable into the overall system without any adverse affects.
- As new hardware sub-systems are developed, they should be able to be incorporated into the core system with minimal software upgrades (mainly at the physical signal interpretation level)
- Must communicate with external legacy systems.
- Must be able to communicate between major components.

The Testing Perspective

The requirements may be in the form of Use Cases or traditional requirements. In either case Use Case based testing will be ideal. If only traditional requirements are used, Use Cases may have to be created. This is a task the testing group could take on.

Functional testing may take place first on a simulator, then on an actual test system.

Proving the architecture will also be important for this project. The test team will have to show that the architecture is layered properly to allow minimal modifications for different hardware configurations. Given the expense of constructing multiple physical test environments, testing the design may be the best way to prove interoperability of hardware components. While the focus of this book is on functional testing, I will cover some aspects of testing the design in the third part of the book.

Experience 3: Aircraft Engine Monitoring System

This project is subject to FAA regulation and shows the impact of working in a regulated environment.

Flying High, an IT consulting outfit specializing in aerospace software, has been awarded a contract to provide control software that monitors vital aircraft engine information for main aircraft control systems. This component is considered very critical to aircraft safety so the certification level for this component will be level A, the FAA's most rigorous.

In this case, the key player is the Project Manager, Dave. He's worked with the FAA many times before, and is a hired gun for the client. Aircraft systems can be killers if they work badly, and the FAA has stiff guidelines about protecting aircraft and air passengers. Dave knows that, as usual, he's in for a rough ride. Testing has to satisfy him first, before anything gets to the FAA.

Flying High is a small company of competent developers. They have a tight deadline for getting an initial version to their client, so testing must begin early. They define two development/testing phases. The first is the prototype phase, the second is the final product phase, a cleanup and rethink following FAA guidelines.

After the prototype development, Dave calls in a third party consulting company, *Down To Earth,* to help get the software certified. The software works and the client likes it, so the task of Down To Earth is to fill in all the blanks to get FAA approval, including the requirements documentation, design, and of course, testing - while changing the code as little as possible.

Down To Earth treats the project as 'build from scratch' despite hoping to make minimal changes to the existing code. They call this a Top Down/ Bottom Up approach - all artifacts take into account the Top (what the customer says they want) and the Bottom (existing code that the customer likes).

When writing requirements they look at the system specs and any client supplied information. At the same time they also talk to the developers and look at code to see what the existing software does. Design takes into consideration the top (requirements) and the actual software. There will be some parallel work taking place. They know they will have to make some changes to the code, but want it to be minimal.

As for testing, the system will have to be tested against requirements and design, and must prove that every line of code was tested and that all existing code is accessed.

The Testing Perspective

In this situation the test team must deal with a high degree of governance. The FAA clearly states their expectations of what it will take to prove the system. This makes understanding what to prove easy.

On the other hand, the list of what needs to be proven is quite extensive. Not only will functional testing be required, but white box testing and code inspections will also make up a large part of the testing effort.

Since a goal is to keep as much of the prototype code as possible, modifications will take place on the part of requirements to match the code. The testing team will have to be aware of potentially changing requirements.

Requirements for projects of this type generally take the form of traditional requirements. Chances are that the test team will have to create Use Cases to group the requirements if they want to do Use Case based testing.

CHAPTER 4

What Is Essential Testing?

Essential Testing: testing the right things, at the right time, to the right level of detail, in the most efficient manner, to prove a software system works and works correctly.

The type of testing we do and what we test to prove that a system works depends on who we are proving the system to: the stakeholders. We do the proving, they assess the proof, and provide the approval. They help us determine the right things to test, the level of test detail, and the proper timing of the tests.

Meanwhile, as testers we have to be efficient as well; being efficient is the key to testing success. If testing isn't done in a reasonable amount of time using a reasonable set of resources, then, as testers, we still fail.

Efficiency adds proactive-ness to testing - being efficient means being aggressive and courageous about testing, while knowing that many aspects of projects won't be to our liking as testers, or within our realm of control.

However, before you can be efficient, you need to know the basics. This chapter explains the basics of essential testing. I'll get into being an efficient tester later. I will finish this chapter by talking about how bad things will happen and how to avoid them using Essential Testing

Testing The Right Things

There are some givens about WHAT we are going to test on every project, no matter the type of project. So, the essential things we will test, and test against, are usually assumed. For example, requirements.

Beyond those givens, the "right things" to test depend on project constraints, and what the stakeholders expect. These fall into two categories: constraints and expectations.

- Constraints are given "givens" such as regulatory requirements, technology standards, architectural gotchas.
- Expectations are more subtle. Typically, the stakeholders that ultimately approve the system are most concerned about what the system does and less worried about how it does it.

In situations where stakeholder expectations are the key proof, testing against what the system does, without being concerned how the system does it, is sufficient. Almost.

For example: a website application where the stakeholder is most concerned with functionality. Testing against requirements may be all that is required to sufficiently 'prove' the system.

But, think like a tester! Just because the stakeholder is happy to see the functionality described in the requirements work as expected doesn't mean that testing is successful, or that you've been a success as a tester!!

It would also be beneficial to perform at least some minimal load testing and stress testing to ensure that something embarrassing doesn't happen when the application goes live and undergoes normal use.

Load testing verifies that the system operates correctly under the environmental conditions the system is expected to face when it is deployed. These conditions include things such as the number of expected users at given times, and transaction volumes. Stress testing simulates extreme conditions the system may face and tests that the system performs to a specified level of performance under those conditions. An example of stress testing would be testing that a system can respond to user requests within a specified response time under specified degraded conditions.

The other extreme… we are testing software that is going into a jet. If the failure of our software causes the jet to fall out of the sky, then the "right things" to test will most likely be different, or at least a lot more!!!.

And, in this case, a stakeholder, the FAA, will let us know. The FAA is a major stakeholder when it comes to guaranteeing public safety in the air, and is going to require some assurance that the software won't crash a plane.

So, with the FAA as stakeholder, there are other 'essential things' to test: specifications, component designs, ensuring there is no dead or deactivated code… and testing every damn line of code.

War Story

Making the Major Stakeholder Happy

Sometimes, unlike the FAA, a stakeholder can expect too little. The Conveyor System provides an example.

The requirements and constraints were rigorous. Bring packages onto a conveyor from multiple lanes, merge them into a single lane with optimal spacing so that they didn't run into each other. Divert them to final destinations without causing jams. Overall, control the flow of packages from one end of the conveyor until they make it to their destinations and are reported on. Typical design constraints included

continued...

allowing for different types of component hardware to be configured into a conveyor at the same time.

So, we have a major delivery scheduled along with a demonstration of functionality for the VP who is the major stakeholder of the project. We create a huge list of tests performed, with results, to present to the VP: component level tests, communication tests, system safety tests and so on.

We present the results to the VP. He just shrugs and says he only wants to see the boxes go around the test conveyor. So we bring him down to the test system and load up the conveyor and watch boxes move at high speeds. The VP is happy with what we may consider a simple visual test.

Obviously, other things must be tested to ensure we created the right product, but as far as the VP is concerned, boxes going around a conveyor without running into each other or falling off are good enough.

(For the next release we still do what we consider necessary testing but keep most of it within the team, and show the VP boxes going around the conveyor.)

Testing To The Right Level of Detail

The right level of detail involves understanding how deeply a product is tested, and thinking intelligently about risks.

The general consensus is that no matter how much time is available, you can always test more. So, testing comes down to how much time you have to test and what you are going to spend it on.

I want to challenge that premise right now. With Essential Testing it is possible to give some of that testing time back by being as lean and efficient as possible while still getting the job done.

Our first inclination when testing is to be afraid. We are afraid we won't catch something important. Based on that fear, we tend to want to cover everything if we can. We also know we can't test everything so we build all kinds of models to help us decide what to test.

Essential Testing says it's okay *not* to use all the time and resources available to you for testing on a given project. If we look at the big picture and how everything fits together, we will get an intelligent understanding of what we need to test.

But, we need to keep challenging our conclusions as well. Rather than asking what else we can test and adding levels of detail, consider what tests can be dropped. If it turns out we made a mistake, we can always change our minds later.

For example, if a product is being tested that uses a communication component that already exists and is being used by other implemented products, there is probably low risk associated with it. The thing is already running successfully somewhere else. Directly testing the component to prove it works would be of little value. Functional black box testing against requirements along with performance testing on the final product is most likely good enough.

Suppose, on the other hand, instead of using an existing component, we are building the communication mechanism from scratch. On top of that we will be using new concepts, new technology, and a team of green engineers (no, I don't mean environmentally conscious). Now we have some serious risk related to that component. Should we change our strategy and test the daylight out of it?

You might be inclined to say yes.

Not so fast.

Barring any responsibility to mitigate embarrassment, I would argue that the strategy is still pretty much the same. Chances are the engineers will do sufficient testing as part of their development. If not, the component will probably blow up when integrated into the product for the first time. We will know something is wrong soon enough. If necessary, we can provide some extra tests to the engineers to ensure that basic commands are being processed correctly by the new component.

There may be some obvious project risks, but the development lead and Project Manager can handle them, and should. We need to trust the PM and engineers, and let them worry about the risk associated with the communication mechanism.

Still, if it looks like those risks may affect us as testers, we may need to be proactive. We need to ensure that the final product works correctly. If there are safety or performance issues related to the newly created component we will need to make sure these issues are incorporated into the testing.

Consider another scenario where the communication component was being built from scratch, but also was slated for use in other systems. In this case we may test the component as a final product. This would entail a whole other level of testing. The level of testing would also change depending on what the final product is being used for and the quality level expected. If the product was safety critical and part of an aircraft, we would give the communication component special scrutiny whether it was built form scratch or previously existed.

Testing At The Right Time

Testing at the right time can't be separated from Testing The Right Things and Testing To The Right Level Of Detail. The kinds of tests performed and the level of detail they test typically depends on the development stage you're in.

Look at the big picture, including the delivery plan - what software gets delivered when. Knowing what can be tested at what time is important. We may test the same thing at different times to different levels of detail.

Use Cases really help understand the timing of tests, even if the development environment is NOT based on the Unified Process or a variation.

When a bunch of individual "system shall" requirements must be verified as part of the entire product, it may be difficult to understand dependencies and the best time to test requirements in conjunction with delivery. Testers can create Use Cases either as interpretations of requirements or as a means of packaging requirements to help in the planning and timing of tests.

The virtues and practical use of Use Cases are detailed in later chapters, but it is worth mentioning something about them here. Use Cases are by nature sequential. They tell generic stories about the uses of a system. These stories help us understand what requirements are *really* important. They also illustrate dependencies - which helps with test sequencing.

War Story

Using Use Cases Regardless

I was tasked with identifying functional tests for requirements of stand-alone components that provided specific services to requesting components. The services of each component to be tested varied in functionality and complexity. Traditional requirements were provided for each component.

I couldn't clearly identify dependencies between requirements. Even though the (traditional) requirements were testable, clear, concise, and all that, I would expect slightly different results depending on the sequencing of other related requirements.

continued...

So, while I could define tests for each requirement individually, I couldn't be sure the expected results were correct. Although I had a clear picture of the individual requirements related to each component, I didn't have a clear picture of exactly what each component did.

What was missing was a sequential description of what the component did in responding to other components. The people who wrote the requirements probably understood these expectations, but I didn't.

My solution? I wound up jotting down Use Cases for components and passing them on to the requirements writers. They could quickly read the Use Cases and tell me if my interpretation of the requirements was on the mark. This made it a lot easier to define tests as well as understand the timing of the tests.

Bad Tester

For Testers, problems occur when we get any of the things I just wrote about wrong, either individually or, more typically all together.

Some of the extreme examples of catastrophes related to improper testing can be that the software kills or injures someone, renders a billion dollar piece of equipment useless, causes a business to make expensive mistakes.

Risky stuff!! But catastrophes are less likely to occur if Testers have a way of focusing on the right things when the stakes are high.

Okay, most problems encountered are less radical.

A typical example is putting too much effort into testing the wrong stuff, then finding out late in the game that there isn't enough time to test the most important things. The major symptom of this is that the testing team just runs out of time.

How to avoid this? The test team manager, armed with the tools of Essential Testing, gets involved with project planning early. And, being courageous ensures that good testing is a priority, not an afterthought.

Frequently, testing doesn't fit seamlessly into the overall development effort. Testing has always been reactive, and it may be seen as a project burden, courtesy of memories of QA overkill, multiple walk throughs, peer reviews and so on. These can provoke Project Managers into testing denial.

Essential Testing is proactive; emphasizing testing agility, timing and being ready to perform the right tests at the right time… helping Project Managers mange projects properly.

Another example: proper things are tested to the proper level, but it can't be proven to the client.

I have seen situations where great care was taken to plan and develop tests, but when the final product was tested, it was still unclear whether the product passed sufficiently. Many times assumptions were made about requirements that were never resolved, or timing of tests were planned that didn't mesh with the context of the delivered product.

All these potential problems can be avoided; most are related to the Tester's ability to understand the project environment and opportunities to adapt.

Essential Testing focuses on understanding the overall process and environment we are testing in. If we start with that understanding, we can plan and execute our testing effort appropriately and avoid most show stopper problems.

CHAPTER 5

Essential and Efficient Testing

Essential Testing depends less on planning - and executing those plans rigorously - than it does on understanding your development environment, creating plans for agility, and then being able to adapt to changing circumstances with efficiency. Efficient agility, if you will.

In this chapter, I will show how the concept of 'agility' - a group of ideas, not a process or a methodology – can be the basis for Essential Testing. I will start by discussing the notion of capital 'A' Agility, and then show how it applies to testing.

Since Essential Testing can be practiced with any of the current mainline development processes (Agile, Unified, Structured), not to mention the most common development process, MixedBag, the actual application of Essential Testing to any of these processes will be described later.

We actually need to look at two separate concepts: Agility, and then Agile Testing. These are very often confused, especially by those in the Agile community.

The Idea of Agility

Currently in the industry there is a notion of 'Agile Testing': the testing practices for projects using an Agile methodology.

In other words, any time you test on a project using an Agile methodology, you are doing Agile Testing.

Agile Methodologies

Of course, there are a *number* of Agile methodologies out there, each with its own set of specific practices:

- Extreme Programming (XP)
- Crystal
- Adaptive Software Development (ASD)
- Scrum
- Feature Driven Development (FDD)
- Dynamic Systems Development Method (DSDM)
- XBreed

Agile methodologies focus on getting the product developed with only the activities that are required. If an activity is not contributing to the end product, then it isn't necessary. The focus is on short iterations that include developing a working product, continuous integration of new components into the working product, lots of team communication, and frequent feedback by stakeholders.

Agile Developers consider themselves 'test infected': infected by the idea that testing early and often will help them write better code. They also like to keep things as simple as possible.

Applying Agile Methodologies to Testing

Agile advocates also have a set of values in what they call a manifesto:

We value:

- ***Individuals and interactions*** over processes and tools
- ***Working software*** over comprehensive documentation
- ***Customer collaboration*** over contract negotiation
- ***Responding to change*** over following a plan.

And, while there is value in the items on the right, we value the items on the left more.

Okay, how could this apply to testing?

The Agile Manifesto is nice, but sounds more like an us-against-them type of thing. Us-workers against them-managers and them-bureaucrats and anyone else who doesn't appreciate the purity of being a developer and the nobility of the work. Maybe even Us-testers at times.

Well, maybe, that's overkill.

But consider just one value: *We value working software* over *comprehensive documentation.* Well of course, what development team player wouldn't? (And how many of you have been on projects where the opposite was true…)

But, is comprehensive documentation itself the opposite of working software? Or is this just a glib idea that sounds cool? The difference may not be interesting to developers, but is VERY important to Essential Testers!!!

As testers, we know that working software and comprehensive documentation certainly *aren't* mutually exclusive; some projects dictate comprehensive documentation because the stakeholders dictate it.

And, also as testers, we need *efficient* documentation because we are trying to get the testing job done in the most efficient way possible. This means satisfying our stakeholders – proving to them that the product works correctly and satisfies *their* requirements, not just the needs of the developers.

These values are fine, and when it comes down to it, just about everyone agrees with them regardless of the type of project being worked on. It's just not many developers are in a position to apply all of these values in any specific project – if at all.

And developers only have to prove themselves to team leaders and project management. Testers have to prove the end product to the stakeholders themselves, in some ways a much bigger job these days!!

So, while Agile values may be a useful counter-balance to the old, rigid, 'high-ceremony' approaches to managing development once necessitated by the cost of developers and hardware, they need agile adaptation outside the limited world of pure Agile Development.

For testers, the neatest concept they provide is the focus on doing the minimum activities required to deliver a quality product and nothing more.

Agile Testing

How Agile Folks See Agile Testing

Most developers see *Agile Testing* as something that happens within an Agile project.

A Tester on a project using an Agile methodology is going to embrace these Agile values and will test consistently with whichever Agile methodology is being used. Since the 'traditional' definition of Agile Testing is testing on a project using an Agile methodology, it is not surprising that Agile Developers think of Agile Testing in terms of the specifics of Agile Development:

- Test early
- Test often
- Test just enough
- Use exploratory testing
- Test to augment an agile development process

Agile advocates like to contrast 'Agile Testing' with 'traditional testing' in ways that contrast Agile methodologies and heavy process methodologies. To them, traditional testing is any testing not on an Agile project. It is about:

- needing finished requirements before testing can begin
- specs thrown over the wall to the testers without explanation
- testing against risks, not needs
- waiting until the end of the project to have the system 'complete'
- a bureaucracy of testing, including reviews and gateways

The result they see is all types of problems because the real result is waiting until the last minute to find out that the system isn't working.

In contrast, Agile Testing proposes testing early and often and addressing defects as they occur, so there are few surprises toward the end of the project.[2] They say, and rightly so, that a heavy process dictates a lateness for testing, and creates a 'testing cycle' that is too late.

The Agile folks are right in important ways. Traditional testing is an outdated approach that doesn't reflect the development realities of the 21st century. However, 'agile' values don't have to be limited to 'agile' projects, and, as I'll demonstrate, they can provide an important contribution to modern testing practices regardless of development methodology.

They need to be expanded on, added to, to reflect the practical experiences of 21st Century testers.

Essential Testing and Agile Testing

Apply Agility to Any Development Methodology

One reason most IT people think of testing in an agile way only in terms of Agile projects is because they don't think it is possible in any other development environment.

I think agility can be applied to any development environment. A little common sense and thought can and does make all the difference in any development context, regardless of the development 'concept'.

This is especially true for testing. Testers have not been part of the development spotlight, and so development processes have treated 'testing' as the potential 'bad boy' of development, needing a firm QA and project management hand for guidance - or as an aspect of programming, needing no guidance beyond the inherent wisdom of all-knowing programmers.

Typically, this has ruled out the idea of 'testing in an agile manner' on projects not using Agile methodologies. Not to

2 "Agility For Testers" Elizabeth Hendrickson, Pacific Northwest Software Quality Conference, 2004

mention thinking about testing in a way that extends 'agility' beyond the narrow focus of Agile Development!!!

I am an experienced tester, test planner, developer, and requirements guy, etc. In other words I've played most roles in a development team. I know Testers have brains and are capable of thought and adaptation. I expect them to adapt agile methods when on any project.

How Essential Testing Addresses Agility

Essential Testing answers an unasked question: Why can't testers adapt agile methods within their environment no matter what methodology they are bound to? It says: Testers should be able to control their job within the development environment, and not be second class development citizens.

So, it's obvious that there seems to be a solid definition of Agile Testing that works for Agile Development. No need to change it. The Agile Process folks got to use the term first, so they have a right to define it.

What Essential Testing does is adopt the gist of their philosophy to provide ways of operating within any process. And, perhaps, suggest ways that testers can add stuff to Agile Testing ideas that makes sense to testers themselves.

Just to repeat (as little as possible)... Efficient Testing is about testing the right things to the right level of detail at the right time in the most efficient manner.

While being agile is an important element, being efficient means taking agile concepts as a starting point only: performing only test related activities that get the job done without wasted effort.

So, no matter what the environment, we should be considering "what is the least amount that we can do to get the job done".

In the case of the tester, that job is to assure that the final product meets certain quality standards are satisfied and presented in a manner acceptable to the ultimate stakeholders.

Essential Testing means we, as testers, work within the spirit of the agile 'philosophy' while accepting that there are bounds we have to appreciate. These bounds define our relationships with developers. And so we have to fit within development process notions associated with "Agile" development, or the expectations of those using variations on the Unified Process, or the mandates of what I'll call the Regulated Environment...

How to fit into all these, and still stay sane as Testers? That's the subject of the next chapter.

CHAPTER 6

Being Essentially Agile

This chapter is about the agile core of Essential Testing and how to apply Essential Testing to bring testing agility to non-Agile projects.

As I discussed in the last chapter, 'Agility' and 'Agile Testing' are existing concepts usually only applied to testing on Agile projects, not testing in an agile manner on other types of projects.

I believe testing in an agile manner is possible in any kind of development, and, in fact, the ideas and practices behind Agile Testing can be extended to establish values and practices that will make testing as a whole a better discipline.

This is what I call Essential Testing.

The agile core of Essential Testing focuses on knowing the environment you are testing in, understanding the expectations of that environment, and meeting those expectations in the most effective, but minimalist way possible. The other values Essential Testing requires are more personal; I'll deal with them later.

Remember, Essential Testing isn't just for Agile projects. Every project can use it.

Essential Testing can work with non-Agile projects because it takes into consideration the environment in which testing takes place and aggressively strives to optimize activities within that environment. So it doesn't matter if your universe is a project using XP or a project using Heavy Waterfall, as long as you are one with it.

Essential Testing says focus only on necessary work product and try to eliminate any unneeded testing activities within the boundaries of the present environment - a concept that can work within any project, because it doesn't scream for radical change.

Rather, it insists on common sense[3], an understanding of what needs to get done, and the courage to get it done as efficiently as possible.

The Agility Basics

Essential Testers know that testing in an agile manner means

- understand what needs to be done
- know the environment
- communicate a lot
- anticipate change
- be a minimalist
- be ready to explain yourself
- oh yeah, don't be lulled into sleepwalking through a project.

The first three are usually project specific; the others are personal best practices. There are three other basics, borrowed from Extreme Programming (XP), and real life:

---

3 "Common sense is a term I am fond of just as I am of "good judgment", mainly because people understand what it mean. Besides, I know the term drives stodgy testing folk crazy. It's not testable.

- Be courageous
- Encourage feedback
- Respect and expect respect

While I'll go into all of them in much more detail in later chapters, here's a brief introduction to each.

Understand What Needs To Be Done

In testing, there are *project* expectations and *product* expectations that determine the level of detail that needs to be tested.

In our Engine Aircraft Monitoring System example, many of the testing expectations related to level of detail are spelled out for us by product certification guidelines. These guidelines are issued by the FAA and spell out what should be tested and to what level of detail for different safety levels.

On the other hand, testing expectations were set at the project level for the Conveyor System Project example. During initial planning the project team specified how testing would take place. Each software release has specific requirements associated with it and the need to support different hardware components. We can make our own determination of what level of detail to use while testing different elements, based on the complexity and criticality of the software being incrementally delivered.

Know Your Environment

The project environment will help decide what needs to be done - or, more likely, what you can do. Testers need to look for boundaries. Eventually, you may have to push those boundaries to get the job done, but understand them first. If I don't truly understand my environment, I can't be agile in my plan.

I once got a fortune out of a fortune cookie that read something like "A gentleman is like water, he molds to the shape of the container that holds him". I always liked that one because it is all about understanding your environment and adapting to it. That isn't conformity; it is just being humble enough to know what you do control and where the limits are on the things you don't. At the same time, understanding those limits also helps in understanding what may change in the environment as well as what changes you have the power to initiate.

Communicate A Lot

Essential Testing requires constant communication, not just lip service. To understand the environment and what needs to be done, efficient, effective communication has to happen from the beginning.

Right up front I want to know what I am up against and the constraints that bind me. I prefer informal communication over formal, but will take it any way I can get it.

So talk to the requirements analysts and the stakeholders early in the project to understand the product and each group's expectations of what it will take to prove the end result. This includes specified expectations, implied expectations, and expectations rolling around in the back of a major stockholder's mind.

Talk to anyone related to the project to get a good feel for the true environment – project management, architects, developers, and the QA folks if QA is a separate function.

If I am the testing lead on a fairly large project I usually spend a large portion of the planning stage walking around talking to people when I am supposed to be planning (okay I do that no matter what my role). But in reality this is part of the planning process.

Expect Change

Understanding what needs to be done and scanning the environment will help you anticipate what may change. This doesn't mean activities must be planned to accommodate potential changes - that wouldn't be agile. Energy shouldn't be wasted on things that may never come to pass. But expecting and anticipating change allows us to have the courage to take action when it does occur – and be ready for it.

Be A Minimalist

Continually think of ways to do less work to get the job done. If you aren't sure whether to include or delete activities, choose delete.[4] If you are flexible, you can always add things later on.

Keeping things simple makes understanding easier.

I once worked with a guy who took great pride in his far reaching vocabulary. He also wrote Use Cases. So, he wrote some Use Cases that were simply poetic. The only problem with them was that nobody could understand them. We had to rewrite them so that they made sense and were practical to use.

Simplicity goes beyond common vocabulary, although simplicity helps make things easier to understand. Beyond that, simplifying things ensures that processes are easy to follow, and documents are clear and concise. Striving for the simplest way to do things helps us be efficient.

Be Ready To Explain Yourself

You need to understand the environment, but the environment needs to understand you. If you are going to ask for things of others, be able to explain why you want them. This includes educating others on the project team on best practices and how doing things certain ways helps the entire project.

There are many ways to be persuasive, but I have found that enthusiasm works best. When I feel strongly about the value gained by specific activities or using certain artifacts, I get enthusiastic. This turns into passion that bleeds through

4 My daughter, the project manager, warned me that if you do this make sure you are not perceived as a Slacker Tester. These are testers that try avoiding work.

and is visible to anyone who gets close. I can't help but show excitement. This excitement is usually contagious and others become open to my suggestions. Of course the passion must be genuine so you really have to believe in what you talk about to be persuasive.

Don't Sleepwalk

Don't get so comfortable with a process that you can sleepwalk through it. There may be similarities between projects, but each one is different and we shouldn't be lulled into complacency by those similarities. What can or should be done differently for each project? Stay on top of the environment and what needs to be done - this will go a long way to reducing complacency.

Encourage Feedback

Feedback is the other side of communication.

With Essential Testing we want to know that we *are* doing the right things. If we are trying to push the envelope we want to know when it breaks.

Feedback comes not just from stakeholders as we find acceptable ways to present test results, but also from other key testing clients including project managers, developers, etc.

Feedback starts early too. Force feedback into your testing process so that you are constantly evaluating yourself. The Agile people like to talk about testing early and often. Well, as testers, we want feedback on what we are doing early and often.

Courage

Courage is not something normally associated with testing, but it is vital to testing success and should be embraced by all testers. Too often I've seen testers in an unending state of fear or worry. They sit on their hands and wait for things to happen. When they see things on the project that could be improved, the stay silent, knowing potential trouble is on the way.

Testing with courage means being aggressively proactive about ensuring the proper things get tested as efficiently as possible. Being courageous requires balancing fears and concerns with confidence. This includes understanding that things won't go as planned, taking action when warning signs appear, and being willing to adjust course when unplanned situations arise.

Risks and problems are normal and too easy to become a focus. In the FAA certification world there are plenty of papers that talk about dangers and pitfalls that should be avoided when creating software that goes into aircrafts. What these papers are short on are solutions to avoiding them.

It is okay to worry. Courage is the willingness to pull your head out of the sand and take action to address those worries. And courage includes the courage to be wrong. If you don't get it completely right the first time, that's okay as long as you understand what needs to be done next and have confidence that you can turn things around when they go sour - without jeopardizing the project.

Respect

This is the latest XP value. In Essential Testing, we want to respect others and their work, and consider that we strive for synergy. This respect also extends to overall goals of the project. This is part of being aware of our surroundings.

Conclusion

Essential Testing shares more than just core concepts and practices with Agile Development. It embraces the significant values behind being agile, and extends them in special ways that have additional meaning to testers.

In the next chapter, you'll see how all of this applies in practice, to any type of project.

CHAPTER 7

Build Testing Agility Into Any Project

It is possible to fit Essential Testing into all types of projects. It's just a matter of knowing the environment and striving for efficiency. To show how, I am going to discuss three types of projects. I'll call these types Agile Iterative, Heavy Iterative, and Heavy Waterfall.

These are *my* types, by the way, and I know they don't cover *all* projects of course. But they help illustrate at a very high level how Essential Testing applies across the spectrum of development types.

Finally, I'll provide more detail on working with safety regulated systems. In theory, these systems can be built using any process, so long as the end results are documented to be of minimal risk. However, depending on the certification level, they require far more testing rigor than normal commercial systems, and so are a special example of how Essential Testing can apply in even the most extreme circumstances.

Agile Iterative

Agile Iterative projects have short iterations that incrementally produce testable product. The focus is less on documentation to support decisions and more on producing delivered software that works and is testable. The product delivered in early iterations is likely to change as the developers add functionality to the product and the stakeholders understanding of the product changes, and consequently the requirements change.

Applying Essential Testing to Agile Iterative

The Agile folks pretty much have this type of project covered. There is less planning up front, with a lot of testing as each iteration is delivered. Early testing is more exploratory where the tester wants to make sure that things don't break and is less worried about detailed requirements testing - if the requirements are going to change, don't worry too much early. Stakeholders will tell you what they do and don't want as they see the product progress.

The Rinkratz example fits into this mold.

Heavy Iterative

Heavy Iterative is more formal. A project following RUP would normally fall into this category. There is more emphasis on planning up front and stability in requirements than is the case with Agile Iterative projects.

Once the planning phase is completed, the product is incrementally produced in iterations. However, the iterations are considerably longer than Agile iterations. They can be treated as mini waterfalls where to some degree you go through Requirements, Analysis, Design, Implementation and Integration, and Test in each iteration.

The early iterations focus on shoring up the architecture and eliminating risks, while it is expected that later iterations, more focused on construction and integration, will run smoothly, based on what was learned from the early iterations.

Applying Essential Testing to Heavy Iterative

From an Essential Testing point of view, a risk to eliminate early on is the risk that the testing process will be too cumbersome and won't adequately convey system readiness to the stakeholders.

In the 'planning' phase make the test planning activities as lean as you can get away with. Focus on doing as little as possible while helping other project roles in the first iteration based on the environment. You can always add more control and activities later as you learn from early iterations since, from a testing perspective, the early iterations are as much a learning experience as anything else.

Later testing within iterations will be more formally focused on requirements and presenting results to stakeholders than in Agile Iterative projects. Still, think lean.

The Conveyor System example would be a Heavy Iterative project.

Heavy Waterfall

Heavy Waterfall is the traditional development process that everyone talks about, where there is tons of documentation and lots of early planning.

The project goes through stages of Requirements elicitation, Analysis, Design, Development and Integration, and Test. This methodology is used quite a bit on large projects where the correctness of the product is a major concern. It is perceived that monitoring and control need to be in place to manage the large number of people working on such a project. Familiarity with the process is another reason it is used.

Critics will tell you that there is too much focus on documentation and not enough focus on development up front. They will also tell you that since requirements will change an early focus on getting all the requirements right is more trouble than it is worth and can lead to a mismatch between the final product and what the stakeholders really want. These are all valid concerns, but the reality is that there is a need for these types of projects and a large number of professionals work on them.

Applying Essential Testing to Heavy Waterfall

There are many adaptations of the waterfall to accommodate some of the concerns, such as having multiple builds and releases of product. Essential Testing would focus on using most of the up-front planning time allotted to get to know the environment. Understanding stakeholders, the project process, and the individuals carrying out the process as much as possible is key.

On many projects that employ Heavy Waterfall a document called a "Test Strategy" is required in addition to a Test Plan. It spells out the *who, what, where, when,* and *why* of testing without talking dates or details. This is used to prove we testers understand the environment and, since/once it gets approved, acts as a CYA.

I discourage using such a document if it doesn't directly contribute to the testing of the product or isn't a required artifact in one form or another. As the Test Plan is built, the info normally provided in a Test Strategy will be gathered anyway. The formalized CYA aspect of this document shouldn't be a major concern for an Essential Tester. Don't forget, one of the basics of being efficient is being able to explain yourself.

The Test Plan should be the leanest and meanest you can get away with. Iteratively identify and create tests cases while working with the requirements people and fostering interaction with the stakeholders.

Since you can't test against requirements up front, focus on understanding requirements early and getting as much stakeholder input as possible. Plan on educating the stakeholders as much as possible on what the final test product will look like and what they can expect. Plan on the minimalist side and let the stakeholders tell you what else is needed to make them feel comfortable.

As the project progresses, and testing is detailed, place more focus on the adequacies of the tests and then on the execution of the tests themselves. There are plenty of opportunities to keep things simple as you trudge toward the ultimate goal.

Safety Regulated Systems (for example FAA D0178b)

Safety regulated systems are typically built using Heavy Waterfall, but worth a more detailed section to themselves.

What Regulated Systems Are

All systems are 'regulated' to some degree, because the standards and rigor related to the product depends on the expectations of the stakeholders.

However, what we think of as *regulated systems* are usually systems that the government has an interest in, usually in the name of public safety. This is even true with financial regulation - think of Sarbanes-Oxley and the legacy of Enron and WorldCom. The usual result of regulations is certification, and a certification process that proves to one or more regulatory bodies that nothing related to regulation was ignored while a system was being constructed.

A couple of regulating bodies that are interested in software certification are the FDA and FAA.

- The FDA is ultimately concerned with health safety and software in the health field that could cause harm to individuals if not implemented correctly. Examples include software that controls blood testing equipment or any equipment that interacts with humans, and software that categorizes and stores health test results.

- The FAA is concerned with flight safety and any software that could cause harm to people in aircrafts. Examples include software that aid in monitoring aircraft traffic, and any software that runs on an aircraft that flies in US airspace.

Certifying Regulated Systems

Regulated system certification isn't just about testing. Testing, and proving that you tested thoroughly, is important, but equally important is proving that you planned development activities, and followed the development process properly.

The testing process dictated in these regulated environments is usually rigorous and rather heavy as you could expect.

Someone responsible for certifying software of this nature must not only be able to verify the software works properly and doesn't cause anything dangerous to happen, but also that a specific process was planned and followed in a defensive enough manner during the lifecycle to ensure safety. Fear plays a part in these processes and justifiably so. But even within these heavy processes there is room for agility in testing at all stages.

Applying Essential Testing to Regulated Systems

Using the FAA project as an example, one of the earliest opportunities to communicate with the regulating authority (the FAA in this case) is through the approval of initial planning documentation. There is one document in particular called the *Plan For Software Aspects Of Certification* (PSAC). This is the document used to tell the FAA what you are building, what level of safety you plan to build into it, how you intend to build it, and what you are going to do to prove it works. This is kind of a strategy for the entire project. Typically this document should be approved before a single line of code is written.

Generally, you don't talk directly to the FAA, but to a person you employ as a liaison between you and the FAA, someone called a *Designated Engineering Representative* (DER). This is the person you use to be your sounding board. As the team builds the PSAC, we can be bold, ensuring that our testing techniques remain as lean as possible. The DER will tell us if we are off the mark and let us know what he thinks will be acceptable.

Since verification includes proving that the requirements are implemented properly, testers must have a good understanding of the specifics of the development process that will be used, and then interpret and communicate their role in an 'essential' way:

- knowing what needs to be tested when
- acknowledging the fear in the back of their minds while not being overcome by it
- and focusing on only what needs to be done without overdoing it.

An important aspect of certifying regulated systems to software testing is traceability.

For regulated systems, traceability is king. In order to prove verification of both process and product, requirements are traced to analysis, design, and code - and tests traced to those artifacts depending on the level of rigor required. This level of traceability doesn't really affect agility of the entire process if done right.

I'll go into details about tracing and tracing artifacts later in the book. But for now, I want to emphasize that tracing can be done well without driving people nuts.

Okay, heavy process can be intimidating. In many cases a company or organization that signs on to develop a product that must be certified isn't prepared for the rigor. They may be provided with system specs and a timetable, but not much else. The requirements for certification include following a heavy process, but typically, these guys are competent developers who don't want to be bogged down. The process seems so overwhelming that the team may just go forward and build the product from the system specs and worry about certification later. This isn't the norm but it certainly happens and often is not accepted by the regulating authority.

Fortunately there are organizations specializing in certification that can help out, that know the industry, are heavy on testing skills, but also strong on understanding process and capable in all aspects of development. They may have to build a process where one isn't apparent, around system specs and code that works. Then, they follow the process as if they didn't have any code, in order to ensure all relevant artifacts are created. From there, testing occurs against requirements and defects are tracked.

Despite working in a regulated environment, these organizations are themselves a good example of 'being essential'. They know what they're up against, based on experience, eliminating a lot of the fear. Depending on the product being developed, they understand what needs to be tested, the level of detail required, and how to best present the results. They also are familiar with the regulatory environment (FAA) and being experienced, can quickly get up to speed on understanding the client environment.

Experience and knowledge of the environment help these specialized organizations put processes in place for handling development and testing that is lean and mean, enabling them to get things done quickly and efficiently.

Conclusion

In this and prior chapters I have defined Essential Testing and made a case for using it whenever possible on just about any project. Now that you understand what it is and how it can be used, I can explore how to put it into action. But remember, each instantiation of testing process and activities for any project should embrace the values of Essential Testing.

The next chapters will demonstrate how to plan and test according to Essential Testing values.

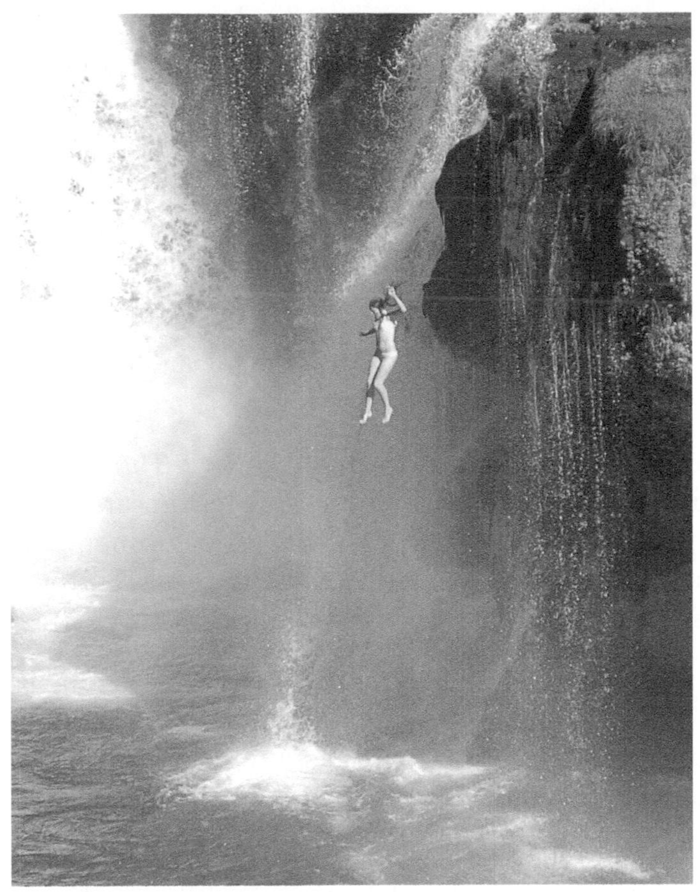

Part Two

Fundamentals For Testing Success

So far I've talked about what Essential Testing is and, along the way, I gave brief explanations of testing concepts.

In this part of the book, I discuss in greater detail concepts vital to doing testing.

Don't worry. This section isn't very long. It will help you become familiar with ideas that become part of the testing process I will discuss in Part 3.

I'll cover

- What good requirements look like and actions that can be taken when they are not so good
- Use Cases and their importance to testers
- My definitions of Test Cases, Test Suites, and Test Procedures
- Building a test process that fits, as a starting point for communication and planning

Requirements are so vital to *Testing The Right Things*, they must be a priority to all testers. Successful testers are dependent on requirements supplied by other development partners, therefore they must be able to tell if these partners have succeeded, and what to do if they haven't.

And I think Use Cases are vital to doing testing right, so I will spend some time defining them from a testing perspective - and, in the process, showing you some examples of good Use Cases, since there are so many bad ones out there.

Also, because there are many different definitions of Test Suites, Test Procedures, and Test Cases, I'll spend some time being clear how I use these terms, and how I think these artifacts can be created in the most useful way.

Finally, the last chapter of this section will cover concepts related to building a testing process that are consistent with Essential Testing. This chapter will lead us into the next part of the book where I will discuss how to do testing beginning with planning.

CHAPTER 8

Requirements–Fundamentals For Testing Success

No matter how obvious it is, I can't stress enough how important requirements are to any software development project and how having good requirements is vital to testing.

Software requirements are conditions or constraints that the software system must comply with, usually broken down into functional and non-functional requirements. In this chapter I'll deal with software requirements from a testing perspective.

In this chapter, I'll explore:

- what good (and not so good) ones look like
- the various forms they may take
- what they are used for
- how requirements, good, bad and so-so, affect testing.

Perhaps most importantly, from a testing perspective, I'll discuss what can be done when requirements aren't so good, and *anticipating* requirements, an important proactive element of Essential Testing.

Good Requirements

Requirements are supposed to drive the entire software project, which is, of course, why they are so important to testing. How can you test if you don't know what you are testing?

Software requirements describe what the system should do: consider them contracts between the stakeholders and the people building the system. So in order to prove the system works as it should, it is important to test against the requirements and prove that the system developed meets those requirements, and satisfies the contract.

Many projects fail because they don't have good requirements. Lousy or constantly changing requirements may sink a project. There are plenty of ways to wind up with poor requirements.

For example, the stakeholders may not have a clear understanding of what they want the system to do. This leads to ambiguous requirements or clear requirements that change constantly as the project progresses. Or perhaps the analysts capturing the requirements didn't do a good job and the folks approving them didn't scrutinize them or didn't care.

Not having good requirements leads to difficulty proving the system either works or doesn't when it is finally complete. Since this is the major responsibility of testing, testers have a vested interest in good requirements. Good and stable requirements are important to testers because it makes their life easier. Essential Testers have a responsibility to do whatever they can to ensure good requirements. I've seen many situations where testers knew early on that the requirements sucked, but didn't say anything. Testers must be willing to voice concern when they see problems with requirements, and must be proactive in taking action to correct the situation wherever possible.

Unclear requirements make it difficult to understand the expected results of the software or even get an understanding of what the entire system is supposed to do. In many situations, requirements do not get clarified until they are implemented. Then, the interpretation of the implementer becomes the final definition, and more often than not the formal requirements definition doesn't change to match the final perception. Not only does this cause testers to struggle to adjust tests at the last minute, there is always a chance the stakeholders won't be happy with the final product even if kept in the loop.

Constantly changing requirements (in effect, poorly managed requirements) also cause grief to testers. Even if everyone agrees with changes, it can be difficult for the testing team to maintain tests after they are developed. Agile folks handle constantly changing requirements by just accepting change as a fact of the project, and moving on. This approach only works because they have immediate access to the stakeholders, can treat the code as the documentation, and may have less bureaucracy to deal with. For them, change management is embedded in the development process.

However, most developers have to deal with more rigid environments.

The reality is that on most projects, not all requirements are good early on nor are all of them stable. We are always going to have to deal with sub-optimal conditions and change.

With Essential Testing, poor or changing requirements are less of a problem; like the Agile folks, we accept the inevitable reality and deal with it proactively.

What Makes Up Good Requirements

A seasoned tester can pick out problems in requirements a mile away. And it doesn't take long to learn. On one project, I worked with a team of testers straight out of college, new to testing. I continuously hammered on the importance of having good requirements. Once they started writing Test Cases against requirements it didn't take long for them to be experts on good requirements.

Here is my standard list of criteria for good requirements, based on industry standards. Good requirements are:

- Clear (Understandable)
- Complete
- Reasonably Detailed
- Verifiable (Testable)
- Correct
- Consistent
- Unambiguous

This isn't a book on writing requirements, so I won't go into great detail about writing good ones. But I do want to discuss my version of good requirements criteria to help you know what to look for.

Clear requirements are requirements that everyone can understand. As a tester, I want the stakeholder who accepts the requirements, the people implementing them, and those of us testing against them to all have the same understanding. The clearness issue can be avoided by getting as many disciplines involved as possible in requirements review. This takes time that not everyone may seem to have, and a consensus on clarity can be difficult to gain. Essential Testers will take the lead if necessary! It is worth the effort to communicate requirements early to foster understanding.

Complete and ***Reasonably Detailed*** need to be balanced. As testers, complete requirements are important for making sure we are testing everything that needs to be tested. At the same time we don't want to go overboard with details to the point that the requirement is difficult to understand. One way to provide detail without cluttering up a requirement is to reference selected supporting details in external documents where possible.

Verifiable (testable) requirements are those that a Test Case can be written against that can validate whether the requirement has or has not been implemented correctly. A requirement is only testable if it has been broken down to a level where it is ***unambiguous***, i.e. precise.

In order to make a requirement precise, specific values should be used in the description of the requirement. Conditions or actions associated with the requirement must be specified. Examples of using specific values include terms such as "90% of all end users" or "product quantity must be greater than zero". Conditions or actions should be stated plainly using terms such as "the user enters data", "the order is validated", or "the check amount is deducted".

An example of an imprecise requirement is "The system must be easy to learn". This requirement would be almost impossible to verify without any specifics. What does "easy to learn" mean anyway? Instead of the above requirements we could write the following. "After 2 days of on-the –job training (defined), 90% of all new customer service employees will be able to view order details and place/modify customer orders with a rework rate (defined) of less than 5%." This is much clearer and we don't have any questions about what to test for.

A requirement is **unambiguous** if all readers read the requirement and understand it in exactly the same way. This gets back to clear requirements. Of course you don't want to go overboard and make a requirement so non-ambiguous that it looks like a legal document. There is a balance between an understandable requirement and no ambiguity at all.

One way to help the balance is to supplement the requirements with diagrams or tables to enhance understandability. Alternatively, consider breaking up OR conditions into separate requirements. If this is done, the sub-requirements must be verifiable and all parties must agree that the sub-requirements accurately represent the original requirement and are acceptable as written.

An example: "When the system receives a 'Low Oil Pressure' message from either the left or right engine, a corresponding Engine Oil Pressure warning message shall be displayed to the main cockpit display." I can understand what this means and the stakeholders probably could as well. But I need to make sure everyone is clear on this and that testers test it correctly.

To clear things up I could write two requirements. One would be "When the system receives a 'Low Oil Pressure' message from the left engine, a Left Engine Oil Pressure Low warning message shall be displayed to the main cockpit display." The other would be "When the system receives a 'Low Oil Pressure' message from the right engine, a Right Engine Oil Pressure Low warning message shall be displayed to the main cockpit display."

Enough about good requirements.

Exactly what constitutes a good requirement is always subjective to some degree, but in most cases, as testers you will know a good one when we see it. You shouldn't be concerned with less than perfect requirements as long as you understand them and know how they're understood by the stakeholders and project team - and you can test them accurately.

Not So Good Requirements

You won't always have good or stable requirements. So, while the focus of testing on an Agile project is testing early and often, testers on other types of projects should focus on the *requirements* early and often.

This means getting involved in reviewing the requirements as early as possible. The level of involvement will vary from project to project but requirements must be addressed by the testers.

Being agile, you will want to get your nose into the requirements as soon as you possibly can on any project. When and how you get involved depends on the project and again on knowing the environment. Ideally, get involved as the requirements are created or, worse case, in the review process.

In some projects, testers will be allowed to have input into the final product. On other projects you may not have any say on the requirements and have to take them once they have been base-lined.

What To Do When Requirements Aren't So Good

Once requirements have been received by the testing team they can be used for identifying and writing tests. As the process of identifying and creating tests begins, it quickly becomes apparent whether or not requirements are good enough, since the major part of identifying and writing tests is gaining an early understanding of the requirements.

What can and should be done when encountering poor requirements depends on the environment. It is important to do whatever it takes to continue to move forward quickly.

Here are two possible courses of action.

First scenario: you have the ability to request changes to requirements once they have been delivered.

Take advantage of this opportunity.

In order to get requirements accepted and changed quickly, suggest revisions and specific changes directly to the requirements managers. This way you know exactly how the requirement will look if it is accepted and you can continue with your activities of creating tests. If your suggestion or interpretation is off base, tweak your test to compensate. But more often than not your interpretation will be accepted if you did your homework.

This requirements help shouldn't be considered doing

someone else's job either. Your attitude as a Tester: it doesn't matter who is ultimately responsible for the requirements as long as they work.

Second scenario: requirements are delivered and you are told they will not be changed further - for example, they are base-lined. But they may be base-lined before they are in good shape.

A way to deal with this: make informal changes to requirements and document them. Write your interpretation of the questionable requirements using input from the requirements managers, stakeholders, or anyone who can help clarify. Document your interpretation and make it known that this is only an interpretation in order to move forward.

The interpreted requirements can be used to identify and build tests. As tests are executed, the tests can be presented to the stakeholders to show the interpretation of what is being tested. Most likely the interpretations will stir discussions that help clarify everyone's understanding of the meaning of the requirements. Then, changes to tests to reflect clarifications can be made as needed.

Remember: Always take the bully by the horns.

Be Proactive: Anticipate Requirements

Even if requirements aren't available early, it may be possible to anticipate what they may be. This can be inexact, but anticipating requirements when none are available can be a key to Essential Testing.

For Essential Testing, testing management should plan to have resources available to a project as soon as possible, even if the project doesn't have a need for them until later. A lack of requirements doesn't mean testers can't plan tests. Sure, it's tough to know what to test when you don't know the requirements. That shouldn't stop you from sketching them out.

Start with any related documentation that talk about the system being built or modified. From there communicate with anyone who will talk to you who you think may potentially, provide some enlightenment.

If the requirements analysts are available, talk to them - try to get a sneak preview of requirements.

Talk to stakeholders. Of course, if you do, make sure not to step on the toes of the requirements analysts and make sure it doesn't look like a duplication of effort from the point of view of the stakeholder.

Document your requirements sketches in Use Cases or scenarios (I'll tell you about Use Cases for Testers in the next chapter!). Use these initial Use Cases to get feedback from people who know about the requirements. From there you can identify potential tests, sketch out Test Cases, and even get an idea of how tests may be implemented.

Yes, this *is* starting early and working against artifacts that are not the requirements, but this is a start, and you will be acting in a proactive fashion. If you're wrong, you can always change things, once the formal analysis is underway. If you do your job correctly, and communicate as much as you can, you most likely won't be far off the mark anyway and, in fact, may be able to contribute to the completion of the requirements.

CHAPTER 9

Use Cases For Testers

Because of their importance as a testing tool, I'll provide a brief explanation of Use Cases here. Since they are also subject to wide variations in the way they get defined in practice, this explanation is intended to help Testers understand Use Cases from the vantage point of a Tester.

> *Use Cases are a way of expressing requirements based on the perspective of users outside of the system. They capture the uses of the system in terms of achieving goals or value for someone or something outside the system. That someone or something outside the system is called an Actor.*

Actors represent roles that interact directly with the system under development. They are external to the system and can be human beings, other systems, or devices.

- Human Actors can be any role a human takes on within an organization that interacts with the system. Examples include Hockey Player and Team Manager in the Rinkratz example and Pilot in the FAA example.
- External system Actors are systems that interact with the system under development through the Use Cases. Examples include Ground System or Central Aircraft Control System in the FAA example.

- Actors can also be inanimate objects. In the Conveyor System example, Package becomes a major Actor since it interacts with the system via sensors and gets value from being transported to the correct location.

Working With Use Cases

Use Cases are depicted with specific model elements and diagrams in the UML, and specified in standardized text.

Use Case Diagrams

Use Case diagrams are used as a static representation of the Use Cases in a system and the Actors outside the system that they interact with. They are a nice way of showing the high level functional scope of a system.

Figure 9-1 shows the Use Case diagram for Rinkratz.

Actors are depicted as stick figures and Use Cases as ovals. Lines between Actors and Use Cases show interaction between the two. In this example I have a dotted line surrounding the system. As you can see, the Actors are outside the system and in this case we have human Actors such as a Hockey Player, Team Manager, and League Manager. We also have Actors that are systems such as the Accounting System, and the US and Canadian Hockey organization systems.

Here's one technical detail that's especially important to note for a tester....

There are two Use Cases, *Set Up a League*, and *Set Up a Team*, both dependent on the *Check Background* Use Case, since those Use Cases can't exist without the *Check Background* behavior. When a user wants to register a new league or team, the user's background is validated to ensure that he/she is a member in good standing with at least one of a number of US or Canadian hockey organizations. This common behavior works the same in both Use Cases and so is separated into the *Check Background*

Use Case. *Set Up A League* and *Set Up A Team* are said to have 'includes' relationships with *Check Background*, that is, *Check Background* is included in both.

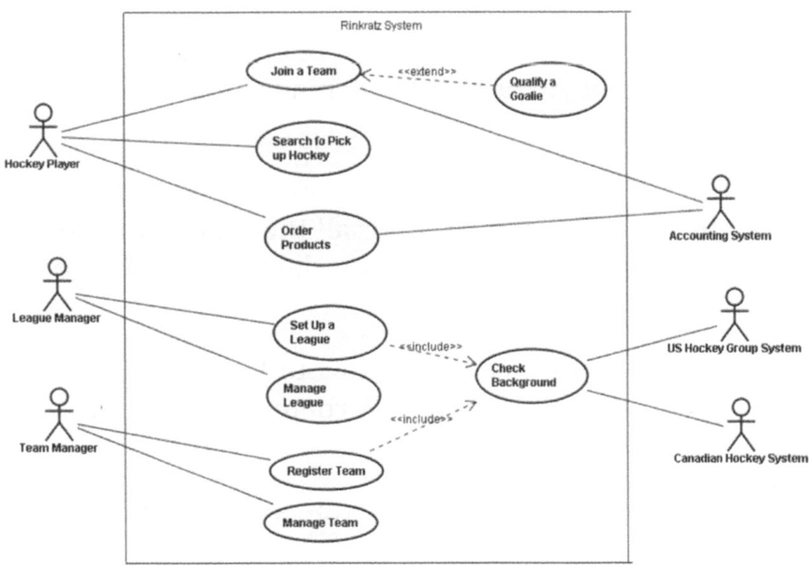

Figure 9-1 RinkRatz Use Case Diagram

Use Case Specifications

A Use Case Specification is the container for the sequential story the Use Case tells: the story of how the system satisfies the goals of the primary Actor.

The real value of a Use Case is the dynamic relationship between the Actor and the system. A well written Use Case clarifies how a system is used by the Actor for a given goal or reason. If there are any questions about what a system does to provide some specific value to someone or something outside the system, including conditional behavior and handling conditions of when something goes wrong, the Use Case is the place to find the answers.

The Use Case Specification shows the sequence of interactions for a Use Case in terms of the Actor. The Actor does something and the system responds. Each sequence of events is written as a flow. There are two main types:

- A main flow describes the interaction between the system and Actor that takes place most of the time to achieve the Use Case's goal.
- Alternate flows are used to show conditional behavior. Alternate flows don't occur all the time, but take place under certain conditions in order to fulfill the goals of the Use Case.

Another type of flow you may encounter is the 'exception flow'. This is a variation on the Alternate Flow, used to handle error conditions.

Use Case Specifications also include other elements most importantly:

- Pre-conditions (These represent the state the system must be in or information that must exist within the system prior to the Use Case taking Place)
- Post conditions (These represent changes in the System State that occur once a Use Case has been executed.)
- Issues and Assumptions (This is a good place to identify any issue related to the content of the Use Case that must be resolved, or assumptions made while writing the Use Case.)

Why Use Use Cases

Employ Use Cases to better understand what a system does. They help us understand the requirements of the system in context. This is a great use, but not the only one.

I like to use Use Cases in every project I work on regardless of whether they are the official requirements or not. If they are not the official requirements, then they are good for grouping traditional requirements and helping to understand how these fit into interactions within the system.

Use Cases In Essential Testing

Use Use Cases in Essential Testing as either the functional requirements or to group the requirements.

- If Use Cases represent the functional requirements, the requirements are found in the body of the Use Case Specification. Each Step of a Use Case flow where the system does something can be considered a requirement that can be tested. These requirements can be tested based on the flow of the Use Case. All main flows and alternate flows in a Use Case should be tested. In Part 3, I detail how Use Cases can be used to identify and select tests.
- If a project is using traditional requirements, Use Cases can still help. Use Cases can be created to group the requirements by functionality. As mentioned before, the testing personnel can create Use Cases for this purpose if they don't exist.
- When grouping requirements by Use Case, traditional requirements can be mapped to steps in the Use Cases they pertain to. This helps show the sequence in which requirements are enacted. Also, a trace from the traditional requirements to the Use Cases makes it easier to show mapping to tests when proving the system works.
- A requirement may map to steps in more than one Use Case. This is fine. As tests are written corresponding to Use Cases, some requirements may be tested multiple

times… which shows that the requirements are satisfied in the context of different uses (Use Cases).

Use Case driven testing provides a way to identify and develop tests that is thorough, flexible, and works on just about any project. Even if you work on projects where there are no Use Cases, when you see how this works you will want to build them if you don't have them.

Perceived Problems Testing Against Use Cases

A common problem cited with using Use Cases to test against is that there isn't enough detail to test properly.

Typical complaints:

- variables aren't adequately defined
- business rules aren't always specified
- the narrative can be ambiguous.

All of these complaints are about poorly written Use Cases, but…

- If you write a decent Use Case you either identify variables in the body of the Use Cases where it makes sense or you reference external documents to maintain readability and understandability. Referenced documentation in turn becomes part of the requirements.
- Likewise, good Use Cases will either include a section for business rules or reference them as separate documentation.
- As for ambiguous narratives, the point of the Use Case is to describe system functionality in a way that everyone can understand. Ambiguity should be out of the question.

The bottom line: a good Use Case should either contain the information or reference the information to adequately test its functionality.

Make 'Em If You Aint Got 'Em

Use Cases are vital to the testing effort. They are the ideal way of expressing functionality of a system in a way that everyone understands, including the stakeholders that are going to accept the system. So if you don't have them you should want them to the point of creating them yourself. If your project doesn't use them that doesn't mean you can't create them or something similar such as user stories or scenarios as part of getting to the final test product. I consider this being proactive as a tester and helping the project succeed.

CHAPTER 10

Building A Test Process That Fits

To start, when building a testing process the essential things are:

- Stakeholder needs and perceptions
- The size of the project
- Project artifacts
- Project activities
- Project synergies
- Minimizing artifacts
- Team dynamics

Test Process: Scoping

Stakeholder Needs and Perceptions

The first priority: the effort put into testing is proportional to the needs of the stakeholders. If you have a lot of stakeholders with different needs from a testing perspective, you have to consider the minimal effort to satisfy those needs. This may take some prioritization.

Consider each stakeholder or stakeholder group individually.

What are their perceptions of what they need to feel comfortable that the product is ready? Does their perception match our perception? Can we and should we change the stakeholders' perception?

It all boils down to what we understand the testing needs are, and what the people approving and ultimately living with the product think, and feel.

We want the stakeholder feeling comfortable, but at the same time we want to focus on spending the testing effort testing the right things to the right level of detail. It comes down to communicating with the stakeholders, understanding their needs and perceptions as they relate to testing, evaluating our own perceptions and balancing the two. This is part of knowing the environment and what we can and should do within it.

In a project like Rinkratz, where there is a single enthusiastic stakeholder who will know what he wants when he sees it, the testing effort can be toned down. This stakeholder, Denny Lemieux, is more concerned with the functionality, look, and feel of the product. He wants a hockey website that will appeal to hockey nuts like him.

Since that is the case, and he is accessible, let him tell you if the functionality is ok. Of course you need to control the process just enough to get Denny to agree on what is good enough and you will have to ensure that the underlying infrastructure will handle the functionality satisfactorily in a live situation.

In the Conveyor Project, we know that, while the ultimate stakeholder, VP Jim Bland, just wants to see boxes go around the conveyor system in an orderly manner, there is a lot more to the testing effort than that. For example, we have to ensure the infrastructure is properly in place to handle inter-operability of hardware.

We also have other stakeholders to think about, such as sub-system providers, and the project architects. And, we have to consider the existing functional and performance requirements. Finally, we have to determine the best way to present test results in a manner that is understandable and meaningful at the same time.

In the FAA project, a major stakeholder (the FAA) will have made most of its expectations clear to us in the form of published guidelines, eliminating a lot of the guesswork. For them, it is mostly a matter of understanding how to present the results as efficiently as possible to match the expectations within the guidelines.

But, remember, we have another stakeholder - the group that hired us, Sky High. Fortunately, as usual, they just want us to meet the FAA's expectations and get the product certified with as little hassle and as little cost as possible.

So understanding stakeholder needs and perceptions in this case is a little easier than in the Conveyor situation. But that doesn't make the overall testing effort any easier, just clearer at the beginning.

Big vs. Small

Another consideration is the size of the project and the overall process that will be employed to get the job done. The scope of the project inevitably affects the testing effort. Larger scope usually means more things to test. More people on the project mean more people to interact with and meeting their needs.

Most of the time, project planners equate project size/scope with testing effort. Essential Testers can help fix that. We know that, sometimes, other factors play a larger role in determining the level of effort going into testing.

The FAA project is a good example of a project that would be fairly small with a large testing effort, because there are other factors other than product scope. Not only the validity of functional and non-functional requirements must be proven, but also a greater level of detail in testing must be shown. On top of that, we must show that we adequately tested design requirements, prove that all code is covered by tests, and that no code is present that isn't being used.

Test Process: Inputs and Outputs

For testers, artifacts are either inputs or outputs. We need to look at both: what we're going to be provided with and what we're expected to produce.

Knowing what inputs are available and the condition they are in will go a long way to understanding how we go about proving the system. There will be different types of input artifacts in various forms. Requirements, design artifacts: these are vital to testing. There may be other artifacts such as source code and standards that we need to consider, but requirements and design artifacts are what we will test against, within the constraints imposed by architecture and stakeholder expectations.

Requirements as Test Inputs

Requirements are what we use to prove the system is correct. What we decide to do with them depends on the type of requirements, the condition they are in and the type of project.

In some cases there may be system specifications that encompass more than just the system we are concerned with. In other word, there are no real clear requirements to speak of. My editor suggests that, when this occurs, we should start exploring dice.com for other opportunities, or maybe cashing in an IRA. Those are options, but there are other options.

First think about the project methodology.

On a fairly small or informal project a system specification may be all that's needed to start with. For example, in the case of Rinkratz, Denny Lemieux will know what he wants when he sees it. Since an agile approach is being taken, there will be close customer contact with short iterations. A concept is all that is needed to start with. You may not expect any formal requirements documentation.

For heavier methodologies, such as iterative/incremental or waterfall, something more substantial will be needed. You would think not having formal requirements on projects like these would be out of the question, but I have seen it happen.

When it does happen, convince others on the project that requirements should be created, or take on the task of creating them yourself.

Testers NEED requirements!!! And GOOD requirements!!!!

Design Artifacts as Test Inputs

It won't always be necessary to test the design. System design is usually a constraint, to be tested *against,* as opposed to requirements, which you test *for*.

For projects where design constraints are not specified by stakeholders, how the system works may not be a factor in proving the system. That doesn't mean design constraints are not an issue for the development team. There will always be design constraints to contend with, often imposed by architects. Those constraints may or may not merit testing.

Remember- know the environment.

It may be up to testers to appease others on the project that the system is sound. Compatibility issues and organizational standards may specify design constraints that must be followed. The tester must understand what will be important to prove.

> *Regulated environments are big on proving the design all the way up at the system level. Regulated agencies, like the FAA and FDA, love 'validation' and 'verification' when talking about software testing. For them it is a major part of software validation. So, to be clear, software verification proves requirements work as stated, validation proves all the requirements were implemented and are capable of supporting their intended use. OR – we did it right AND we did the right thing.*

Where aspects of the design must be proven, you need to know what design artifacts are available. They can take various forms: System Architecture Documents (SADs), formal design documents for heavier projects, even informal documents.

Worse. Informal documentation - or none at all - for less formal or Agile projects.

Depending on the development process, the artifact notation may vary. For testing purposes understand the form the design artifacts are in, the condition they are in, and what will need to be done to adequately test the design.

Outputs

What artifacts that must be produced - for example Test Cases, automated tests, bug reports, and test results, as well as intermediate artifacts that are used to get to the final products. These may be determined and shaped by the testing tools available. The expectations of the stakeholders and the project also determine what artifacts must be produced to prove the system.

Projects employing heavier processes may expect formal reviews to ensure the testing effort is adequate. Controls may be placed on artifacts such as baselining tests.

Again, the least amount of output artifacts to adequately prove the system is preferable.

Shaping The Test Process

The artifacts available, the condition they are in, and what has to be done to produce the expected outputs - these all shape the project testing process.

But, as courageous testers you may need to add activities to get certain artifacts up to snuff so they can be used in an efficient way.

An example: I was on a project where requirements were presented in the form of Use Cases but written by developer types with no history of writing Use Cases. The "Use Cases" presented were nothing more than sequence diagrams that went into great detail on the inner workings of the system, but didn't lend much about the true functionality the system provided, or the interaction between the system and the outside world.

We were expected to do black box testing and were not allowed to request changes to the requirements. We planned on using a simple process for identifying and developing tests based on Use Cases, but knew the existing requirements were not sufficient. To compensate we added activities, writing unofficial Use Cases as interim artifacts, getting the stakeholders and requirement writers to agree on the content.

Normally, adding activities and artifacts to a project process isn't consistent with being agile, since cutting activities is better than adding them. In this case adding the activities was being agile. We had a very efficient process for developing tests that required good Use Cases, so adding activities actually made the overall process more efficient.

Part of being agile in testing is being able to see the big picture, understanding what will make you more efficient, and doing what it takes.

Understand Project Needs

Translation: understand the project and the project 'process', and where testing fits into the scheme of things.

Synergy with the rest of the project team is very important. We want our testing processes and artifacts to blend with the expectations of the rest of the project. This also requires an understanding of the tools and artifacts preferred by the project. These will vary depending on the project environment.

Here's an example of fitting the testing process into the needs of the rest of the project.

In the FAA project, the third party, Down to Earth, is given a clean slate by Sky High in order to get the final project certified with the FAA.

Down To Earth knows Sky High is very comfortable with traditional requirements, and that Sky High is using a low cost requirements management tool. The project has decided to create traditional requirements but asks for the testing team's input in deciding which requirements management tool to use.

The testing team normally uses an automated requirements management tool that works well for traceability but chooses to recommend the one Sky High is familiar with when they found it would still be able to manage traceability. The test team also recommends that Use Cases be created to supplement the formal requirements, but was willing to create them as part of the testing process if needed. This compromise was done in the name of allowing the overall process to work smoothly. The testing process would have to be adjusted, but could fit comfortably into the overall process.

Plan For The Minimum Artifact Set To Get By With

Focus on the minimal set of artifacts that the test team can get by with and still make the stakeholders happy. In the set of artifacts defined for a project most emphasis should be placed on deliverable artifacts.

Deliverable artifacts will include anything that must be provided to stakeholders or other team members. The objective is to minimize these artifacts.

One question to ask about each artifact is if the project can be successful without the deliverable. The next question to ask is what would happen if the deliverable wasn't provided.

You get the picture. We want to get into the habit of questioning the need for every artifact we produce, and then whether they are long term or interim artifacts:

- Interim artifacts are artifacts that must be created as part of getting to the final artifacts that must be produced, but can be discarded, or more importantly, will not be maintained. We streamline interim artifacts as we establish the testing process.
- Long term artifacts impose an implied long term commitment on the part of the user: they will be maintained.

We create interim documents for efficiency, quality, or just to ensure communications. They should be created only if they contribute directly to the creation of the final test product. For example, on a project where requirements are in the form of traditional requirements, Use Cases may be an interim artifact created by testers in order to do Use Case based testing.

Team Dynamics

Here, the focus is on the interaction between the test team and the rest of the project team. Not only are you trying to make things lean for testing, but you are concerned with making things work smoothly for the rest of the team.

It doesn't matter how agile testing individuals are and if they are testing the right things if they screw everything up for the rest of the project team. You need to make sure you understand what is expected of the testing team from the rest of the project. This is part of knowing the environment and building a testing process that works within it.

Delivery

How will the product be delivered for testing and when? Much will depend on the methodology being used. Projects employing iterative/incremental methodologies are expected to deliver product toward the end of each iteration. Projects employing a waterfall methodology may chose to deliver multiple releases in order to spread out the functional testing.

Things To Worry About

Don't waste time worrying about anything.

Part Three

The Successful Testing Process

In this part of the book, I discuss the *how* of Essential Testing: a roadmap with specifics - what you test (and how you decide what to test, the essential activities that must take place, and packaging the results, with examples.

As I explain all of this, I will make it plain how the basics of Essential Testing can be applied. As covered in chapter 6, these include:

- understanding what needs to be done
- understanding the environment
- communicating,
- expecting change,

- being a minimalist,
- explaining yourself, and
- encouraging feedback.

And, of course, the golden rule: build a testing process to fit a particular project, being as efficient as possible while focusing on the right things to test.

I'll deal with thinking about a test process for a project in order of the priority of the topics to consider. My priorities will help you understand how Essential Testing differs from traditional thinking about testing, keeping in mind the basics above.

I'll cover

- Test planning, and only planning enough to get you started
- Shaping requirements to ensure testing success, including how to use Use Cases to help succeed, whether you have them or not.
- Test selection and design, using a pattern and procedure I've helped develop that simplifies and organizes the tester's job
- Test execution – doing it
- Then, proving it, via traceability and test coverage
- With a word or two about test automation - tricky to implement, this can cause more problems than it is worth if not done properly.

These aren't the technicalities of testing. Rather, because successful testers are dependent on the successful execution of other development partners, testers must have as a starting point a basis for knowing whether these partners have succeeded, and what to do if they haven't.

CHAPTER 11

Essential Test Planning

Test planning doesn't have to be formal, but it must take place. And it doesn't have to be elaborate.

Just do the essential planning; the planning needed to get the job done. Do it because you need a starting point to get off the ground early on.

Later, change the plan - it becomes a guide.

Since testing agility is a goal, don't put too much emphasis on sticking to the plan. To be agile, you must be prepared to change the plan as the project moves forward.

As Essential Testers, who want to get the testing job done in the most efficient way possible be prepared to the point that makes sense, expecting circumstances to change, not being afraid of change, and doing whatever you have to get the job done most efficiently when circumstances do change.

Test Planning Realities

If anybody tells you they can accurately plan an optimal test process, they are either lying, or they overestimate themselves.

You can't imagine how riled I get when someone accuses me

of not sticking to a plan. I never intend to stick to the plans I make – but I develop them like I intend to.

You know things will change, so you need to think 'change' when you plan. You do test planning to attempt to solve the problem of testing on a project. The problem isn't solved when the plan is accepted, but when someone with authority (customers or stakeholders) says they are satisfied with the results.

Early in any project, a Test Plan is devised. The intent is to encourage you to understand the testing problem as best you can. You present what you think is the best approach to solving the testing problem.

This gets you started. As the project progresses, the plan is used to guide the testing team in solving the problem: proving the system. But it should be changed and refined as much as is practical as time progresses. So, creating a plan *is* useful.... But following the plan is less important than adapting to changes in reality from your initial perception. With Airborne Systems you can even tell the FAA you didn't follow the plan – so long as you document what you DID do and include that information in the Software Accomplishments Summary.

Now, you're probably asking - why put much effort into test planning if you aren't going to follow it anyway?

The Essential answer: you take planning seriously so that you understand what needs to be done *and* have an approach to doing it, so that, when some of our initial perceptions are found to be inaccurate, or things change, you can make educated decisions on what to do next.

Who does the test planning? That depends on the project.

On small projects it could be an individual tester who plans his own activities and informally lets the project lead know what he intends to do. In larger projects it may be the job of a single test lead. If a test team is formed early enough it may be helpful to get as many testing personnel involved – at least informally - in the planning as possible. The more everyone understands what has to be done initially, the easier the effort.

Test Planning Tasks

So how do you do serious test planning in an agile manner?

Three test planning activities should take place no matter how informal the testing process or how small the role of testing on a project. How much or how little ceremony is associated with these activities depends on what it takes to get the job done. But, as usual, when in doubt, lean toward less rather than more.

I call these test tasks **understand, analyze, and create**. The first activity is about learning and understanding what testing needs to get done and what has to be presented as results. The second activity is analyzing what is available to get the job done, and the last activity is creating the testing plan.

Planning Starts With Understanding

Early in a project you must be comfortable that you understand what needs to be done, what artifacts are available as inputs, and what minimal outputs are required of the testing effort to get the testing job done. This is the first step to sensible test planning with the bulk of the effort anchored on communication. I have already mentioned some virtues of communicating early and often. It helps the planning process by getting good understanding early. This is also part of understanding the environment in which testing will take place. You need to communicate in order to understand the following things.

- What it will take to prove the system
- What input artifacts are available

- What we can do about them

Understand What It Will Take To Prove The System

Remember, it is important to communicate as much as possible with the stakeholders to understand their expectations of what will prove to them the system works or doesn't work. Documentation and organization policy help, but there is also the human factor to consider.

Many times an influential stakeholder will have to be satisfied in a particular way that the system works, that may not always seem practical. Getting a feel for what is important will help you understand what level of testing needs to take place, what things to focus on, and how to present proof that the system works or doesn't.

Even in environments where there is a lot of guidance on what to test and to what level of depth, there is still a human factor to consider.

Let's take FAA regulated systems as an example.

The FAA has specific guidelines on what must be tested but, as I mentioned earlier, each project seeking FAA certification must have a liaison called a Designated Engineering Representative (DER) who acts independently to interpret guidelines and sort out what is acceptable to the FAA. This position holds quite a bit of power. Even though regulations are fairly clear, the DER may only be comfortable with specific processes or artifacts.

So, know up front what a DER is comfortable with and what he/she is not.

On Object Oriented projects I like using UML artifacts such as Use Cases and sequence diagrams to determine tests for the requirements and design. I also know that most DERs dislike them, or worse. That doesn't stop me from using those artifacts in my test planning, it only changes how I present test and traceability results.

Make sure you know what stakeholders are influential, and what human factors must be considered to prove the system.

- For the Rinkratz example, when we find that all Denny Lemieux needs to be satisfied is the ability to search for places to play hockey, we focus on presenting that while also testing the other requirements.
- For the Conveyor System, if the VP, Jim Bland, needs to see packages cruising around the conveyor system without running into each other or falling off, we make sure that visual 'confirmation' is part of the acceptance test. We will also test all the functional and non-functional requirements to ensure the system really does what it is supposed to, especially with some of the architectural requirements.
- With the FAA example we have specific guidelines to follow that tell us every (high level) requirement must be tested, the design (low level) requirements must be tested, and code not only must be covered by the tests, but it must be shown that there is no dead code. So we know that we not only have to show whether or not each test passed, but that the tests cover all requirements, design, and code. We have to show traceability of requirements to design, code, and tests and prove all code is being executed by the system in fulfillment of identified requirements.

Understand What Input Artifacts Are Available

Often projects are fairly clear on what artifacts are to be produced. So, just looking at project planning documents and organization standards will be enough to get an understanding of the environment you are working in and what artifacts are available to you.

However the artifacts that will be used may not be so clear. They may be suggested, but optional.... and, let's face it, not all projects are that organized. Or a project structure may be out of the norm of what the organization normally does. It is important to talk to the project manager and team leads to see what they expect to produce.

As I've said before, start by focusing on requirements. What form will the requirements take? What containers will hold them? What models will be used to show design?

For example, Use Cases may be supplemented by a specification containing non-functional requirements. Or, requirements may be traditional and the project may have specific standard documents for them. There may also be requirements dispersed in design documents, various models, and interface specifications.

Who is responsible for requirements? In some organizations, all requirements are under the ownership of requirements analysts. Some organizations distinguish between functional requirements that fall under the requirements analysts while the architect or design team is responsible for non-functional requirements. There may be other combinations of requirements owners.

Knowing who is responsible will help us understand how much influence we will have ensuring the quality of what we will receive or the form they are presented in.

Understand What Can Be Done With Artifacts

Once you know what to expect for input artifacts, figure out what you can do with them.

You're not always going to be happy with what you get.

Doing Essential Testing, the aim is being agile within the environment. That means not accepting what you're presented with without any thought or happily incorporating inefficiencies into the testing process.

It also means being proactive and practical.

Essential Testers first compare the current artifacts with the artifact inputs that would make the testing process most efficient. From there they try to influence artifacts form and quality. Depending on how much influence they have, what's the next step?

The obvious proactive one: decide what to do with the available artifacts to help get the job done efficiently. Remember, as testers we need to be pushy.

- If I need Use Cases to optimize the testing effort and they don't exist, I am going to want to build them myself.
- If the requirements aren't clear enough to test properly I want to fix them. But messing with other people's artifacts is a touchy subject and must be handled with care.

Remember, first talk to the artifact creator and see if you can help update/upgrade the artifacts. Not possible? Try introducing interim artifacts to supplement the existing ones. Then, talk to the project manager early and see what options you have dealing with artifacts that are unsuitable or unavailable. Different projects have different policies for dealing with requirements Find out what can be changed or adjusted, but also what should or could be done under the radar.

War Story

Dysfunctional Requirements

I worked on a large dysfunctional project where we wanted to do Use Case based testing - in fact the stakeholder wanted us to do it too.

The problem? The requirements people were also developing the software and didn't know how to write good Use Cases.

continued...

The Use Cases that were written were terrible. They were sequence diagrams that were really part of the design that they called Use Cases.

These 'Use Cases' detailed what happened inside the system. Each sequence diagram was accompanied by a table of operation names describing the steps of the sequence diagram. That was it.

There was no way we could use these things to test against as they were. The engineers/requirements analysts insisted that since these had been base-lined (without input from the test team) that they wouldn't be changed. The project was already falling behind and the project manager wouldn't help.

We approached the lead engineer and reached an agreement where the testing team would write real Use Cases but couldn't call them Use Cases and he would review them to help ensure accuracy. On top of that we couldn't tell anyone these Use Cases existed. As far as anyone knew, these were just interim documents that the testing team was creating to help create tests. It wasn't pretty, but it was the best solution available and it helped us get our job done.

Another war story

I worked on a project where we were given traditional requirements to test against from a client. These requirements had already been base-lined before the testing team ever saw them; many were unclear.

Although we could create any other artifacts we wanted, such as Use Cases, to help us test, the requirements couldn't be changed and the tests had to map to them. The client was in another country and wasn't very accessible to discuss requirements.

continued...

We created a document listing the unclear requirements, and our interpretation of what they meant. As we delivered the preliminary Test Cases to the client for approval we included the document. That way the client was clear on our interpretation; we could continue to get the job done without waiting for answers. If the client said our interpretation was wrong, we would change the Test Case.

Both of these examples are uncharacteristic. However, as testers, we often find ourselves dealing with artifact situations that aren't the best. No matter, as Essential Testers, we can find a solution.

After Understanding, Analyze

Once you know what you're stuck with, you ask what you can do with it to get the job done. So, go to your bag of tricks, and a repository of patterns.

Bag of Tricks

The first question: how do we intend to prove the system? You know what features and requirements are important to prove from understanding the environment. Now you have to consider how to make the case that the system does or doesn't work based on stakeholder criteria.

For Rinkratz, you already know that the search for hockey venues feature is important to the stakeholder. You may decide to present semi-formal testing results for the search feature including load testing. For the rest of the system it may be sufficient to present Denny Lemieux with access to the entire Rinkratz site and let him poke around. Since the development process is agile, he will get the chance to play as new features are delivered with time to make changes.

In the Conveyor System, it is important to identify the artifacts that will be presented and the types of tests run in addition to the visual acceptance test desired by the stakeholder.

In the case of the FAA project, the general format of the artifacts to produce to prove the system is spelled out. It is important to consult with the DER to ensure the FAA will be comfortable with the specific format of the test results.

Next, think about interim artifacts and specific processes. Often you have specifics in mind that you know will get the job done. As you gain testing experience, you accumulate techniques and artifacts that work well under various circumstances: a bag of tricks.

Of course, as Essential Testers, when you reach into your bag of tricks you only pull out the minimal set that will get the job done in the most efficient manner. You understand your environment and the minimal artifacts you must present to prove the system, and select the artifacts requiring the least effort.

Patterns

I consider patterns part of a broader bag of tricks that others use and have proven that they work.

Patterns were formalized by Christopher Alexander back in the 1960's and 1970's as ways to help people who design things (initially real architects) solve recurring problems.

A pattern describes a problem and its context, and provides a means to solve the problem that has been proven to work. Patterns provide a shared language for problem solving, focus on the underlying causes of problems, and provide a venue for creative problem solving.

The software community has adopted patterns as means to create a body of literature to solve recurring problems encountered throughout software development. Patterns in the software development community were initially used to solve software design problems but have spread to other aspects of software development.

Now patterns have crept into the realm of testing.

Brian Marick is right on when he makes the statement that "testers lack a useful vocabulary, are hampered by rigid 'one size fits all' methodologies, and face many problems whose solutions are under-described in the literature."[5] - one of the reasons for this book and also a reason that testing patterns are starting to materialize.

Robert Binder has presented a number of patterns that are a good starting point for testing[6]. I use a modified version of one of his patterns later in this book to present a straightforward means of identifying tests.

But be careful.

When you look at patterns you have to look at the context the problem lives in and the perspective of the author. You may find a situation that looks like yours or possibly solves a real problem, but one that is not necessarily the one the author describes. You may have to modify some patterns to meet your particular needs. Do your own thinking as well.

And, try rolling your own.

Creating A Testing Solution

As you plan, you may encounter situations you haven't dealt with before. You may have to create processes or artifacts from scratch or piece together parts of other solutions to meet your needs.

---

5 Brian Marick, http://www.testing.com/test-patterns/index.html

6 Robert Binder, Testing Object Oriented Systems: Models, Patterns, and Tools

Bring The Pieces Together

You have a feel for what the testing effort needs to focus on and what you need to present for success determination, and an understanding of components for a potential solution. Now you have to put that potential solution together.

Sketch it out first. Keep it as lean and as simple as possible; only consider activities that directly relate to getting the job done. Don't put major effort into finding a good solution at first. While you put the plan together, solutions will become clearer as things fall into place. The Test Plan is just a starting point to get your thoughts together. And, it will change anyway… the plan is a roadmap of what can be done, not what will be done.

Start by laying out the breadth and depth of tests to be performed and the final artifacts that will be presented to the customer. From there identify steps and activities that will take you from the inputs to where you want to go.

When identifying activities and artifacts, be a minimalist: focus on doing as little as possible to get things done correctly. Present the decision maker with enough information to make an un-regrettable decision on the acceptance of the system. Strive to provide nothing more and nothing less while only producing artifacts and activities directly related to that goal.

Chapter 12

Grouping Requirements With Use Cases

You Need Use Cases to Be Use Case Driven

The activities and techniques described in the rest of the book deal with Use Case driven testing. So naturally Use Cases will be needed. Once you've reviewed the requirements and know you understand them thoroughly, make sure good associated Use Cases are available.

If Use Cases are the main source of requirements, you're almost there.

If traditional requirements are the official requirements but Use Cases are provided as a means of grouping requirements make sure the requirements trace to the Use Cases. This will help in tracing requirements to tests later on.

If traditional requirements are the official requirements and Use Cases are not provided, build them yourself. I can't stress how vital Use Cases are to understanding the system and other forms of requirements just don't seem to cut it.

Variations are possible, ranging from formal Use Cases to scenarios, even user stories. Personally, if the traditional requirements are understandable, I prefer simple Use Cases with just enough detail to get by. I include pre-conditions and post-conditions - information needed to start and complete our tests.

A brief description is nice to have too - at least sketch out the steps to identify the system inputs and how the system responds to those inputs

The Problems With Testing Individual Requirements, and Why Use Cases Are The Solution

First, you may think you have all requirements covered (and you may), but testing each requirement doesn't mean the system works correctly.

Reading through traditional requirements to get a handle on what the system does can be cumbersome - and so, you can miss the point on a lot of requirements, especially detailed requirements without a concrete process to tie them together. You can wind up with conflicting requirements that don't get discovered until late, or not at all. Conflicting requirements can occur when the system context in which two or more requirements take place is not adequately explained.

Use Cases help by making logic of the overall use and functionality of the system. Use Case based testing focuses on the real value gained by the system and allows us to present the results to the stakeholders in a manner that they understand.

If you have Use Cases as your requirements, you can get a clear picture of what the system is doing and a sequential dialog of what is happening between the outside world and the system. These Use Cases can be supplemented by other requirements that can be tied to steps in the Use Cases. As testers, the Use Cases provide a scenario to test against. The supplemental requirements tied to each Use Case can be tested along with the functionality. Tying supplemental requirements to Use Cases is done by matching Use Case functionality to individual non-functional requirements that support that functionality.

If you have Use Cases that are *not* your requirements, but used as a way of grouping requirements you get the same thing - a sequential picture of what the system is doing in plain words or simple diagrams.

War Story

I worked with a small team on a project to build a prototype software application to track military personnel in the field. The requirements the team had to work with were data-centric - all about what type of data was to be provided. I asked the team if they needed help with some Use Cases to get a better feel for the interaction with the system and the functional value presented to the users, which were going to be all branches of the military. They declined the offer feeling they had enough information and that eliciting the requirements from stakeholders with limited accessibility would slow things down.

Testing was done based on the requirements that specified what type of data on individuals would be tracked and how it would be presented. The system was built, tested, and presented to the military. It worked fine for the Army, and the Air force and Navy could live with it, but the Marines hated it. It turned out that the Army was very data focused and liked the product because lots of things were being captured and reported on.

The Marines were infantry focused, and already had a system of tracking individuals in the field that relied on a human chain of relationships and responsibilities. The proposed product didn't match their goals of using a system and didn't show any measurable value. It didn't fit their particular environment.

But it passed the tests against requirements.

Use Cases clear up a lot of concerns. First, as requirements are tied to Use Case steps you get a feel for the context each requirement operates in. As I mentioned before, sequence can be seen easily, which may lead to the discovery of conflicting requirements that may look compatible, but can be seen as incompatible in the context of the sequence they are activated. Telling the system story can help make difficult to understand requirements understandable.

Either by using Use Cases as the primary requirements, or using them to group traditional requirements, by allowing Use Cases to drive testing, you have a basis for building Test Cases. You can build multiple tests based on the Use Cases and activities within them.

Example of Grouping Traditional Requirements With Use Cases

Let's take a look at a simple example, a subset of the Conveyor System. I'll use a group of requirements for assigning diverter lanes to specific destinations.

The Business Context

- Packages on a conveyor system must be diverted to lanes leading to loading docks based on their ultimate destination.
- Multiple lanes may connect to a single destination, e.g. a warehouse or a store. There is a business rule that states each truck will have a single destination
- Trucks parked at different loading docks may be going to the same destination.
- A corollary: packages sent to different lanes can end up on trucks going to the same destination.
- Lanes are assigned to a destination and then the destination is assigned a truck which implicitly assigns a lane to a truck.

Initial System View

In assigning *Lanes,* the software associates *Lanes* with *Destinations* - it must have the smarts to choose a lane for each package so that the package ends up at its designated destination. The software may have to choose between multiple Lanes, because of earlier activity assigning *Lanes* to *Destinations* and *Trucks* to *Lanes*. The choice will be based on business rules around optimizing package flow. Optimization depends on how many packages a lane can handle in a given time (lane capacity) primarily, although other dependencies may become apparent.

There are some givens.

The software knows how many packages an *Assigned Lane* can handle, i.e. the limit to the number of packages that can be handled by an assigned truck, based on information previously entered during the assignment of a *Lane* to a *Truck*.

So, when a truck becomes full, the system detects that the lane to that truck has reached its limit. The gate from the conveyor to the divert lane is then physically closed; packages are no longer diverted to that lane so long as the currently associated truck is full.

When a truck leaves, *Shipping Clerk* accesses the system to make the lane available. Later, when an empty truck arrives at a vacant loading dock, *Conveyor Operator* assigns the Lane to a Destination – the destination assigned to the empty truck – and opens the gate to that lane so packages can be diverted to the lane with the new truck.

Understanding The Requirements

For this example, as a Tester, I am concerned with two main requirements:

- assigning available lanes to destinations

- physically opening lanes so that packages can be diverted

Essential Testing Analysis

I construct business scenarios to help understand what can really happen. Here's one simple example: an empty truck pulls into the loading area.

- Driver tells Dock Attendant Truck's destination.
- The Dock Attendant acting as a Conveyor Operator accesses the Conveyor Control System to assign an available Conveyor Lane to Destination combination. Conveyor Control System provides information on available lanes which lead to specific loading docks.
- The Dock Attendant acting as a Conveyor Operator, selects available lane, the destination to assign it to, and the amount of packages that can be diverted to the lane before the truck is filled. Based on the lane assigned leading to a specific loading dock, the Driver is told the Loading Dock for his/her truck.
- Conveyor Operator coordinates opening gate to Assigned Lane. Packages bound for associated destination are diverted to the loading dock associated with that lane.

Supplied Software Requirements: A Sample

Here are some of the static requirements you would typically be faced with, given the business needs identified above. The list is deliberately simplified… okay, some may consider it an example of Extreme Simplification!!

Note: when software requirements mention *the system*, they refer to the software controlling the actions of the physical conveyor system

SRS 1: The system shall limit the number of lanes that may be assigned to a given destination to a number specified for that destination at system initialization.

SRS 2: The system shall display lanes assigned to a destination upon request.
The system shall display available lanes upon request.
The system shall identify that a lane is available if it is not currently assigned to a lane and is not being held for future use.

SRS3: The system shall allow only available lanes to be assigned to a destination.

SRS 4: The system shall allow only available lanes to be held for future use.

SRS 5: The system shall provide the user with the capability of associating available lanes to destinations.

SRS 6: The system shall provide the user with the capability of opening a physical lane gate on request.

SRS 7: The system shall designate a gate as "Opened" when the corresponding physical gate is opened.

SRS 8: The system shall designate a gate as "Closed" when the corresponding physical gate is closed.

SRS 9: The system shall only open a physical gate when that gate is assigned to a destination.

SRS 10: The system shall notify an operator that a gate is locked when a physical gate could not be opened.

SRS 11: The system shall determine that a gate is locked when it does not respond with an 'open' signal within 10 seconds of an open command.

SRS 12: The system shall store gate/destination assignment once an assigned gate is determined to be "Open".

SRS 13: The system shall send gate/destination assignment to the dispatch system when a gate is determined to be assigned and open.

SRS 14: The system shall only assign packages to a lane if that lane is open and assigned to a Truck.

SRS 15: The system shall stop assigning packages to a lane once a configurable, predefined limit has been reached.

SRS16: The system shall be ready to control diversion of packages to a lane once the lane becomes open/ assigned.

SRS 17: The system shall accept destination identification numbers only as five digit numbers

SRS 18: The system shall accept lane numbers only as 4 digit numbers

Requirements Sample Considered

These requirements are, obviously, part of a much larger group. But, for Essential Testers, even within the context of the larger group it may not be completely clear how the requirements fit together. In fact, with a larger group of static requirements representing a more complex portion of the system, it will probably be more difficult to understand how requirements fit together.

But, understanding how requirements fit together is an Essential Tester responsibility!!

So, in this example I need to talk to team members who know how the system is supposed to work - requirements analysts and system experts and Subject Matter Experts (SMEs). Then, as I've said, as I become familiar with what the requirements really mean, I might want some of them changed, or at least stated more clearly. And, again, if I can't get the requirements I don't like changed, I have to document my interpretation of requirements I am unsure of. Yup, CYA, but good testing practice!!! I know, I've talked about all of this before, defining the role(s) of an Essential Tester. Now I can explain some specifics!!!

For example, the requirement, SRS15, stating "The system shall stop assigning packages to a lane once a configurable, predefined limit has been reached." isn't really clear. It talks about the condition when the system stops diverting packages to a lane; the scenario I described is about assigning lanes.

So, I talk with the requirements analyst and a system expert and find that the requirement really doesn't belong with this group - but it *is* indirectly related. As part of assigning a lane to a destination, the Conveyor Operator must specify how many packages can be diverted to the lane. More specifically the system needs to know how many packages can be diverted to a lane before a truck is full.

I find that there is no requirement like this. One is written:

The system shall accept and recognize a value associated with a lane/destination assignment representing the maximum number of packages that can be diverted to the lane.

The original requirement is removed (from my subset, anyway – it may be used elsewhere). The new requirement is added to the group as SRS 75.

Getting To Use Cases

In my example Use Cases are not provided, so I have to create them.

For Essential Testing, this is the next step. Again I have to communicate with requirements analysts, system experts and SMEs about what the system does, if these folks are available. Realistically, I may have to just dig in and start writing Use Cases as best I can, then get someone to read them and confirm what the system really does.

A Use Case Example

Here's what should result: a basic flow for an *Open a Lane* Use Case with alternate flows identified.

I've left the details of alternate flows out for the sake of simplicity. In real life I would probably fill them in.

Open a Lane Use Case

Primary Actor: Conveyor Operator

Secondary Actors: Dispatch System, Divert Lane

Precondition: Conveyor Operator is logged onto System.

Post Condition: Lane is assigned to a valid destination.

Basic Flow

1) Conveyor Operator requests System to open a lane.
2) System prompts for a destination.
3) Conveyor Operator enters destination requested.
4) System displays lanes currently assigned to the requested destination and the lanes currently available.

   Alt: Invalid Destination

   Alt: No lanes available
5) Conveyor Operator chooses a lane to assign to the destination and specifies the maximum number of packages that can be diverted to that lane.

   Alt: Hold Lane
6) System assigns the lane and prompts to open the gate on the conveyor associated with the lane.
7) Conveyor Operator requests to open the gate.

   Alt: Wait to open
8) System responds by sending a request to Divert Lane to open the gate.

9) Divert Lane notifies System when gate is opened.

10) System: Stores the gate and destination information. Sends Dispatch System the lane and destination assignment information indicating packages can be assigned to the lane. Notifies Conveyor Operator when successful

Note: Repeat steps 5 – 10 to assign multiple lanes

11) Use Case ends.

This Use Case gives a clearer picture of how the Conveyor Operator can assign lanes to a destination and ready the system to divert packages to these newly assigned lanes. It helps us prepare for identifying and selecting tests.

For example, I have Conveyor Operator as the Primary Actor and Divert Lane and Dispatch system as Secondary Actors. So, now I have clearly defined system boundaries. All three Actors are outside the system. The Primary Actor interacts to achieve a goal, and the Secondary Actors interact in order for the Use Case to successfully achieve the goal of the Primary Actor.

The next thing I do: map traditional requirements to Use Case(s). Okay, this is an optional step. Depending on the number of requirements you're dealing with you can opt out of this activity.

Like I said, I like to be a minimalist when I can, but there is value to this activity. As you move further through the process and identify tests based on Use Cases, the mappings can help in determining test coverage of traditional requirements.

As mentioned in chapter 9, mapping should be done at a granularity that makes best sense for the project. Sometimes, map to specific steps. Sometimes, map to the Use Case.

Here's an example of mapping requirements to Use Case steps and alternate flows.

Req. ID	Traditional Requirement	UC Step
SRS 1	The system shall limit the number of lanes that may be assigned to a given destination to a number specified for that destination at system initialization.	4
SRS 2	The system shall display lanes assigned to a destination upon request.	4
SRS 2.1	The system shall display available lanes upon request.	4
SRS 2.2	The system shall identify that a lane is available if it is not currently assigned to a lane and is not being held for future use.	4
SRS 3	The system shall allow only available lanes to be assigned to a destination.	1, 2, 5, 6
SRS 4	The system shall allow only available lanes to be held for future use.	5 Alt: Hold Lane
SRS 17	The system shall accept destination identification numbers only as five digit numbers.	3, 4, 6
SRS 18	The system shall accept lane numbers only as 4 digit numbers.	5, 6
SRS 5	The system shall provide the user with the capability of associating available lanes to destinations.	6
SRS 6	The system shall provide the user with the capability of opening a physical lane gate on request.	7, 8
SRS 7	The system shall designate a gate as "Opened" when the corresponding physical gate is opened.	9, 10

Req. ID	Traditional Requirement	UC Step
SRS 11	The system shall determine a gate is locked when that gate does not respond with an 'open' signal within 10 seconds of an open command.	8, 9 Alt: Gate Not open
SRS 9	The system shall only open a physical gate when that gate is assigned to a destination.	7, 8, 9
SRS 10	The system shall notify an operator that a gate is 'locked' when the associated physical gate can not be opened.	8, 9 Alt: Gate Not open
SRS 12	The system shall store gate/destination assignment once an assigned gate is determined to be opened.	10
SRS 13	The system shall send gate/destination assignment to the dispatch system when a gate is determined to be assigned and open.	10
SRS 16	The system shall be ready to control diversion of packages to a lane once the lane becomes open/assigned.	10
NEW SRS 75	**New**: The system shall accept and recognize a value associated with a lane/ destination assignment representing the maximum amount of packages that may be diverted to the lane.	5, 6

Table 12-1 Example of Requirements Mapping to Use Case Steps and Alternate Flows

This is a small list of requirements, but you can see how they map to Use Case steps.

Mapping to Use Case steps work for grouping large amounts of requirements. The mapping strategy and the tools used are up to the project. But, like I said, map just to the Use Case if that's the agreed-upon strategy within the project.

Chapter 13

Extending Use Cases For Testing

Once you have requirements available and Use Cases are ready as described in the previous chapter, the next steps are to identify the potential tests and select the ones to use.

I had the opportunity to work with David DeWitt on a number of projects where we were tasked with coming up with testing plans and processes. Together, we put together and refined a simple Use Case driven approach to test identification and selection that has worked well for us. It works so well that we use it on all projects where we do testing whether Use Cases are official requirements or not. We've even used it on highly regulated FAA certification projects with large amounts of traditional requirements. We found it helps align requirements with tests and illustrate test coverage well.

In this chapter I will cover the first part of the test identification process: identifying operational variables. In the following chapter I will cover the second part: Identifying tests.

Some Definitions

Before I let you in on the details of this approach, you need to know the definitions of a few more test-related terms.

Condition

Definition: ***A distinct value or range of values of the system or for inputs into the system that defines a unique testing situation.***

For example:

An **input** into a customer service application is *Customer ID*.

So, a **condition** for Customer ID would be a valid ID that is associated with an existing customer recognized by the system.

Notice I identify the value in general terms. You don't have to give the input a specific value.

Operational Variable

Definition: ***An input into the system by an Actor that causes significant system response.***

Although all Operational Variables are inputs into the system, not all individual inputs are Operational Variables. Only inputs that cause system behavior to change. Inputs can be aggregated to a broader system input that causes significant behavior. Let's look at an example where the customer search functionality of a customer service system is being tested. The requirements specify that the system will be able to search for customers based on full name combining first name and last name. Although first name and last name are entered into the system as search criteria, neither are Operational Variables on their own. The system bases searches on the entire name rather than one or the other. So the Operational Variable will be Name. First or last name on their own won't change system behavior. If either first or last name is invalid, the system treats the entire name as invalid. It doesn't matter that the entire name is delivered into the system in two pieces.

Note: Sometimes an input (Operational Variable) by itself will not cause a significant response. But when combined with other inputs, the result can be specific system behavior that can be tested for, and needs to be covered. So, each combination of inputs (Operational Variables) should be testable to some expected result defined by requirements.

An example: for the *Open A Lane* Use Case where *Destination ID* is passed to the system by Actor *Conveyor Operator* (step 3). Under normal operating conditions, entering a valid *Destination Id* should cause the system to display lanes currently assigned.

Look at the Operational Variables for *Destination ID* and *Lane Selection* in Use Case step 5 in combination. There are multiple responses the system will have depending on combinations of input values. So besides the specific system response for Destination ID by itself mentioned above, there is a system response when a value is entered for *Lane Selection* as well, in combination. This combination needs to be tested.

(By the way, outputs are *not* Operational Variables - they are a result of system behavior rather than a cause.).

War Story

I was once instructing a team on Use Case driven testing and one tester kept insisting that he needed to treat a specific output to another system as an Operational Variable. His reasoning was that the output caused behavior in another system that in turn caused a change in behavior in the system under test. After tracing the flow of events I was able to convince him that even though the system output from another combination of Operational Variables set off a chain of events, it was really an input from the external system that caused the new behavior.

System State

Definition: *The condition of the system at the start of a test - the stable state waiting for input.*

In the example of testing the system response to a value entered for Lane Selection, one System State would be: "*The system is operational and at least one lane is available for selecting*". That would be the condition the system is in when that test starts. Conversely, another System State could be: "*The system is operational and no lanes are available for assignment*". You can see how starting the same test with the two different System States should result in different system responses.

Important to remember - after processing a set of inputs in an individual test, the system ends up in a new stable (output) state after (correct) inputs have been (correctly) processed.

The state of the system before a test is performed is a precondition of a test while the state of the system after a test has been performed is a post condition.

A post condition of one test can be used as the beginning System State (precondition) to another test. Testing one step of a Use case begins with a System State and ends with a System State. If the next step in the Use Cases is being tested, the ending System State of the test of the previous step should be the beginning System State of the next test.

Discovering System State for tests is iterative that is best done after identifying Operational Variables as part of building variant tables to identify tests. I will explain the steps in the next chapter.

Nominal Tests

Definition: *Tests that verify specific outcomes communicated by the requirements.*

There are two types:

- **Positive Nominal Tests** cover input conditions that are part of normal operation.

An example - testing a function of a system that searches for a customer.

- **Negative Nominal Tests** cover conditions where something happens in the system under test that is not considered part of normal operations. (In FAA terms – these are "Robustness Tests.")

Even though these can be 'unhappy' conditions where something bad happens - or at least not what normally would happen – they are still considered nominal if requirements exist that describe the expected system response to the unhappy outcome.

What is an example of a negative test? Testing a customer search function with inputs outside ranges specified by requirements and that the system responds to as the requirements specify.

Off Nominal Tests

Definition: *Tests that the requirements don't cover, for example, they test situations that the requirements do not specify outcomes for.*

Okay. Off-nominal tests are usually negative tests. And, when I say negative, I mean really negative. (Again – in FAA terms "Robustness Tests.")

These are identified tests that the requirements do not cover, for example, they test situations that the requirements do not specify outcomes for. As part of the test identification process I will discuss shortly you will see how tests can be discovered that describe conditions where system response is not specified by requirements.

These really try to break the system. Many conditions identified by off nominal tests may be oversights on the part of the requirements analysts. Often these conditions can be resolved with a little communication with requirements analysts and developers before testing takes place.

The Extended Use Case Test Design Pattern

The approach David and I used so successfully is loosely based on the *Extended Use Case Test Design Pattern*, authored by Robert Binder, as a means of dealing with what Binder perceived as test-related problems with Use Cases: he sees Use Cases as inadequate requirements.

Of course, I *don't* consider Use Cases as 'inadequate' requirements. Just the opposite… they can be the basis for creating and packaging good requirements regardless of development approach, and modern Testers need Use Cases to do their job properly!!!

As I said in chapter 13, patterns can help solve specific IT problems. But, you need to treat them as a starting point and adapt them to fit specific needs. I've loosely incorporated the *Extended Use Case Test Design Pattern* into Essential Testing as a good starting point for thinking about Use Case based test design and development.

So, let's look at Binder's pattern and why it needs adapting.

Binder's Premises:

Use Cases as requirements either don't or may not hold enough information to easily identify tests for sufficient coverage

Entry points, or inputs, into the system are not always clear

Those entry points often don't have enough information about data and parameters surrounding them.

Essentially, Binder suggests Use Cases aren't testable as is.

Okay, I don't buy that. At least, not if they are written properly. Since Use Cases describe the system from a user perspective in a manner that should be clear to everyone on the project, they should be good enough to test against.

Sure, with Use Cases, there are no specific rules that say you have to describe in detail every variable or where to put business rules. You need flexibility when you write a Use Case so that it is understandable and that requirements analysis is 'agile'.

A good Use Case will be readable, and will have the appropriate level of detail within it, or will reference those details.

But, I love his solution, anyway!!

The Extended Use Case Solution

His solution: "extend" Use Cases to make tests easier to identify and implement. Specifically, he says, define input/output relationships, identify Operational Variables and combine them to create an Extended Use Case table that identifies unique tests. (note: he is not discussing the UML notion of a Use Case extends relationship where one Use case represents optional behavior of another Use Case.)

Binder's solution helps with coverage concerns. In particular, it provides a way to ensure proper test coverage. By following his pattern you can see all potential tests needed for proper coverage of the system, and select the tests necessary to prove the system to stakeholders. Binder's pattern really shines in providing a mechanism to ensure coverage and facilitate traceability when faced with a large number of requirements.

But, the big reason I love his pattern is because it helps you simplify testing in environments that don't look so simple.

Adapting the pattern

David and I modified the pattern slightly to suit our needs. First we added a step to identify and table the Operational Variables as a precursor to identifying tests in a variant table. This just formalizes the process of identifying Operational Variables and makes test identification easier.

We also place an added emphasis on System State, combining it with Operational Variables to select unique tests. This adds another dimension to test selection where the state of the system at the beginning of a test can figure into system behavior.

The Essential Test Identification Approach

Here's an outline of our approach for identifying potential tests from Use Cases based on Binder's pattern:

- Identify Operational Variables: Inputs and Input Combinations
- Package potential tests using combinations of System States and Operational Variables into variant tables

The rest of this chapter shows a simple way to identify Operational Variables to be used to identify potential test. Identifying the potential tests will be covered in the next chapter.

Identifying Operational Variables

Start by reviewing the Use Case that will be the source of potential tests, examining each flow of events.

Whenever the Actor does something, there is a definable input. Every step that describes an Actor initiating an action is an entry point, or input, into the system. Each entry point is a potential Operational Variable. If specific input values "cause" significant system behavior, it should be considered an Operational Variable - I like to treat all inputs as Operational Variables on the first pass and then reevaluate.

As you identify Operational Variables place the results in a preliminary table like table 13-1. It has a column for identifying the Operational Variable name, a Use Case step column identifying the step where the Operational Variable is active, a description column to describe what the Operational Variable is used for, and a Conditions column to identify possible values for the Operational Variable.

Op Variable	Step	Description	Conditions

Table 13-1 Example template of Operational Variable Table

Discovering Operational Variables Example Based on Open a Lane Use Case For The Conveyor System,

I'll use the *Open a Lane* Use Case for this example. Here it is once more.

Basic Flow

1) Conveyor Operator requests System to open a lane.
2) System prompts for a destination.
3) Conveyor Operator enters destination requested.
4) System displays lanes currently assigned to the requested destination and the lanes currently available.

   Alt: Invalid Destination

   Alt: No lanes available
5) Conveyor Operator chooses a lane to assign to the destination and specifies the maximum number of packages that can be diverted to that lane.

   Alt: Hold Lane
6) System assigns the lane and prompts to open the gate on the conveyor associated with the lane.
7) Conveyor Operator requests to open the gate.

   Alt: Wait to open

8) System responds by sending a request to Divert Lane to open the gate.
9) Divert Lane notifies System when gate is opened.
10) System: Stores the gate and destination information. Sends Dispatch System the lane and destination assignment information indicating packages can be assigned to the lane. Notifies Conveyor Operator when successful

Note: Repeat steps 5 – 10 to assign multiple lanes

11) Use Case ends.

The first time an Actor initiates an action on the system is in the first step, where the Conveyor Operator requests to open a lane. This is treated as the first Operational Variable because it will cause the system to respond by (normally) opening a lane.

Create an appropriate name, one that describes the action or input into the system; in this case "*Open Lane Request*". The description for this operational variable: "*This is an input into the conveyor control system to request initiating activities to assign a lane to a destination and physically open the corresponding lane*".

Enter the name, the description, and the corresponding Use Case into the first line of the table - the first entry. Continue to identify the rest of the Operational Variables in the basic flow in the same manner.

Once all potential Operational Variables have been identified and entered into the table, identify conditions for each.

As mentioned before, these are values of Operational Variables that cause a variation in the expected results of the system i.e. that change system behavior. These values may stand alone or work in conjunction with values of other Operational Variables to produce specific system behavior.

For each Operational Variable, look at the Use Case step in

which it is used. Then, look at the corresponding system response for condition values. Condition values can include valid data with different variations, invalid formats, and no data among other things.

When listing variable conditions, start with positive conditions expected within the flow of events in a Use Case, followed by variables that could cause alternate flows to take place, and then values that could cause error conditions or could be considered for negative testing.

Again, let's look at the example table for *Open Lane Request.*

In particular, looking at potential inputs that would initiate a normal system response, there only seems to be one, which is a "valid request". So "valid request" becomes the first value in the condition of *Open Lane Request.*

There are no alternate flows identified in the Use Case for steps one or two where the *Open Lane Request* is present, so there are no potential values that could cause variants in flow. Still, looking for values that may cause system behavior, I come up with two more when considering inputs that may cause error conditions.

These are "invalid request", and "no request".

It is still unclear if these would either be possible or if they would really cause the system to behave differently, but list them as conditions in the table anyway. At this point you are trying to come up with values without scrutinizing them in any great detail. You can do that when you identify potential tests.

The results of this effort are shown in table 13-2.

In my example I identified *Lane Selection* and *Package Limit* from step 5 in the Use Case. This is because the Conveyor Operator is expected to select a lane to assign and a package limit - two separate variables that must be inputted into the system.

Also, note that when I identified the conditions for each Operational Variable, I specified values I *thought* would cause significant behavior. I am not sure all values identified will cause significant behavior at this point, and that is to be expected. These values are identified just to get started identifying potential tests.

An example of this is Operational Variable *Package Limit*. Right now I don't know if there is a range in which the package limit must fall. There are no requirements specifying one at this time or if the package limit value could be 0. I put values for above range, below range, and 0 anyway. Later, I would ask a system expert or requirements analyst about this.

The table in this example should be sufficient to be used in the next activity, selecting potential tests. In that activity we will combine values related to different Operational Variables along with System State to identify unique tests.

Op Variable	Step	Description	Conditions
Open Lane Request	1	input into the conveyor control system to request initiating activities to assign a lane to a destination and physically open the corresponding lane	Valid Request, Invalid Request, No request
Destination Id	3	The destination the Conveyor Operator intends to assign a lane to.	Valid, invalid format, Nonexistent destination
Lane Selection	5	Represents the lane intended to be assigned to a destination	Available lane Held Lane selected, Assigned lane, Invalid lane, No lane selected
Package Limit	5	Represents a numeric value limiting the number of packages that can be diverted to an assigned lane	Valid format, Value above high range, Value below low range, Value of 0 Invalid format No value entered
Open Gate Request	7	Request by Conveyor Operator to coordinate activities to physically open a gate on the conveyor associated with an assigned lane.	Valid, Invalid format, Wrong gate specified, No command

Table 13-2: Example of Operational Variable table for the Open a Lane Use Case

I just explained identifying and Operational Variables. In the next chapter I will show you how to put them to good use. I will describe a means of identifying potential test based on combining Operational Variables and System State.

Chapter 14

Identifying Tests

Once Operational Variables for a Use Case flow have been defined, identify potential tests. Each potential test will be a combination of specific values for System State, the Operational Variables and expected results.

What does that really mean??

When we're identifying tests, we're actually instantiating Use Case flows. I hope you remember - Use Cases are generalizations of *scenarios* - specific ways of achieving some value for an Actor by using the system. So, the instantiations of Use Case flows that we base our tests on are really scenarios. This truly *is* Use Case driven test selection.

In identifying potential tests, I'll use the Extended Use Case Design Pattern that I've discussed before, combining different values for System State and Operational Variables in a new table, the variant table. In this table, each row will identify a specific potential test.

A sample variant table is shown in table 14-1.

These are only 'potential tests' because once the combinations are identified, not all will be kept as tests. Later, I will explain how to select tests by evaluating potential tests against testing goals, requirements, and most of all, what is important to the stakeholders.

Overview

Okay, to summarize.

Identifying potential tests means defining variant paths for each Use Case flow (i.e. significant scenario) by taking unique combinations of System State and Operational Variables and plugging them into a variant table.

Each unique combination of System State and Operational Variables triggers significant system behavior.

Here's what's supposed to be in each row of a variant table, column by column (take a look at Figure 14-1).

First, a sequential number (variant) as an identifier. No 'intelligence' here! Just sequencing!! Each row in the table is a potential test. The identifier is used as a reference when selecting Tests, creating Test Cases etc....

Next - System State. System State is first because it is the state the system is in as the test begins.

Operational Variable - After System State, each Operational Variable has a column. Sequence specific Operational Variables in the order they show up in the Use Case flow.

Then, a column for Expected Results, the outcome for each test variation as defined by a row.

Finally, Comments - any questions or assumptions related to a potential test.

Variant	Sys State	Op Var1	Op Var2	Op Var3	Op Var4	Expected Results	Comments

Table 14-1: Extended Use Case Variant Table Template

Organizing A Variant Table

Before filling out the variant table you must set it up first. You do this by populating column names in the variant table with the Operational Variable names previously identified using the steps outlined in the last chapter.

Here's my layout for a variant table for the *Open a Lane* flow (table 14-2), using the Operational Variable tables created previously in chapter 13 Table 13-2.

Variant	Sys State	Open Lane Request	Dest ID	Lane Selection	Package Limit	Open Gate	Gate Response	Expected Results	Comments

Table 14-2: Variant Table Structure for Open a Lane Use Case Basic Flow

Sadly, as you can see, the table is barely manageable -we have a lot of columns. It could be broken into two tables to make it easier to read.

In fact, here's an informal Rule Of Thumb - if there are more than five Operational Variables, think about using multiple tables for a single Use Case flow. Each table would include a subset of the Operational Variables still sequenced in the order they show up in the Use Case flow.

I am not going to break the table up for this example but I will talk a bit about how it could be done. Here's a brief description of how *Open A Lane* might be split into two.

A good place to split the table is between *Package Limit* and *Open Gate*.

Why?

Package Limit is the last input for the steps leading up to assigning a gate, and *Open Gate* is the first input into the steps related to coordinating the physical opening of a gate.

So the first variant table would include columns for *System State* (as usual), *Open Lane Request, Destination ID, Lane Selection,* and *Package Limit*. The second table would contain *System State* followed by *Open Gate* and *Gate Response*. System state will be used in the second table as it was in the first to identify the system condition that is required to test each combination of Operational Variable values.

But, breaking up tables is hard to do. I have a detailed example and explanation in Appendix B. Like I said, I'll stick with a single table to explain the potential test identification process, to keep things as simple as possible.

Filling In A Variant Table

The focus of this activity: incrementally combining specific inputs for a Use Case flow and specifying an expected system response.

The steps:

- Enter values for combinations of System State and Operational Variables that represent unique scenarios of the Use Case, flow by flow.
- Then, define expected results in each row to create a potential test.

Here's a closer look....

Start with the values for the basic flow of events, adding inputs (aka Operational Variables) as they appear in the Use Case flow.

Once all variants with the optimal beginning System State are covered specify values for each additional System State, incorporating Operational Variables for each.

And here's an example using the basic flow of the *Open a Lane* Use Case.

The first System State should be the state the system must be in to positive test the Use Case flow. In the example, this is "*Operational – Lanes available*".

The first Operational Variable is *Open Lane Request*; the optimal value would be 'Valid Request' - at this point I only want to test the condition of *Open Lane* request being valid. So, the rest of the Operational Variables are not applicable here – I place N/A in the row as values for them. I identify this row as Variant 1, the first potential test.

What this test does is validate the system response when a request is made to open a lane *and* the system is operational *and* lanes are available for assignment. So, the expected result from the Use Case is "The system prompts for a destination."

I put that in the expected results column for variant and now the first potential test is complete. The result can be seen in the table 14-3.

Variant	Sys State	Open Lane Request	Dest. ID	Lane Selection	Package Limit	Open Gate	Gate Response	Expected Results	Comments
1	Operational – lanes available	Valid Request	N/A	N/A	N/A	N/A	N/A	The system prompts for a destination	

Table 14-3 Example of first row in the variant table

I continue to fill in the table.

First I refer to the Operational Variable table to exhaust all values for the first Operational Variable keeping the same System State. These values will typically generate negative results or trigger alternate system behavior.

In my example, the other potential values for *Open Lane*

Request are 'Invalid Request' and 'No Request'. I talked to the requirements analysts and discovered:

- The system doesn't act when there is no request so that is not a possible input value.
- It is possible to have an invalid request but there is no requirement that says what the system does in response.

So the second variant in the table will have the same System State as the first, but I enter a value of 'Invalid Request' for *Open Lane Request*. For *Expected Results*, I indicate we don't know what happens yet. In the comments section I explain that there isn't a requirement yet so this would be an off-nominal test for now. This is the second potential test, Variant #2.

Once I exhaust the values for the first Operational Variable combined with System State, I combine values for it with those of the second Operational Variable, continuing until I exhaust all combinations. Then I start combining the third Operational Variable and so on.

When I've exhausted all System State and Operational Variable combinations I have a variant table that can be used as a set of potential tests. Again, I say potential because now the table must be reviewed to determine if all combinations are really needed, which tests can be combined, which are duplicates, and how much coverage is really needed.

Table 14-4 shows partial results of my example. I am only showing portions of the variant table here since the entire table is very large. The entire table can be found in Appendix B, table B1.

I want to emphasize some key aspects here.

First as you can see, the list of potential tests can get long. For this simple flow I identified 28 variables. There may be more to be identified with a closer look, but this is good enough for this example.

Variants 1 through 24 all include the same value for System State. I exhausted all combination of Operational Variables with the initial state before moving on the next significant value. I walked incrementally through the Use Case flow, combining values for Operational Variables for each step. Variant 22 represents the Happy Path of the entire Use Case flow where all Operational Variables contain values allowing the most common path to successfully complete.

There are also variants where we don't know the expected result because either the requirements are not clear or there are no requirements specified for the condition. Enter Comments to explain what is being done about them.... If possible, go to the system experts and requirements analysts to get these variants clarified and resolved.

Variants 25, 26, 27, and 28 are examples of System State that, when combined with "positive" values for Operational Variable, can cause negative system results.

Var.	Sys State	Open Lane Request	Dest. ID	Lane Selection	Package Limit	Open Gate	Gate Response	Expected Results	Comments
1	Operational – lanes available	Valid Request	N/A	N/A	N/A	N/A	N/A	The system prompts for a destination	
2	Operational – lanes available	Invalid Request	N/A	N/A	N/A	N/A	N/A	Not specified	No requirement yet. Consider an off nominal test for now
...									
21	Operational – lanes available	Valid Request	Valid	Available lane Selected	Valid	No Command	N/A	The system waits for an open command	

Var.	Sys State	Open Lane Request	Dest. ID	Lane Selection	Package Limit	Open Gate	Gate Response	Expected Results	Comments
22	Operational – lanes available	Valid Request	Valid	Available lane Selected	Valid	Valid	Gate Open	The system: Stores the gate and destination information Sends the Dispatch System with the lane and destination assignment information indicating packages can be assigned to the lane. Notifies the Conveyor Operator	
…									
24	Operational – lanes available	Valid Request	Valid	Available lane Selected	Valid	Valid	No response	After ten seconds the system determines the gate can't be opened and informs the operator	
25	Operational – all lanes held or assigned	Valid Request	N/A	N/A	N/A	N/A	N/A	The system informs the operator that there are no lanes available for assignment	
…									
28	No Communication with Dispatch system	Valid Request	Valid	Available lane Selected	Valid	Valid	Gate Open	Not sure what the response is	No requirement

Table 14-4 Open a Lane Basic Flow Variant Table

Conclusion

I just outlined a way to identify tests based on Use Cases, a simple way of identifying tests for complex systems. The key is to focus on System State and inputs into the system, combine values for those variables, and build a table of unique tests to choose from. This gives you the potential tests.

In the next chapter I will describe my definition of a Test Case, and cover how to select tests to run by grouping tests into Test Cases. Then I will explain how to define selected tests in the body of the Test Cases.

Chapter 15

Essential Test Cases

David DeWitt and I also came up with a different approach to Test Cases that better suits Use Case based testing.

Traditionally Test Cases are a description of conditions and expected results that taken together test an individual requirement or a step in a Use Case. This definition varies, but it boils down to defining an individual test by inputs and expected results. Essential Test Cases differ from this in four ways.

- First each Essential Test Case combines multiple tests into a single Test Case.
- Secondly they base test definition on a scenario or flow through a Use Case. It is the best way to be Use Case driven in testing as I will explain later.
- Third, they go beyond test definition to include test design. [I figure since I am defining the test, I may as well define how it is performed. That way, all the information needed to create the test can be found in a single place.]
- Fourth, as if that isn't enough bastardization, I take it a bit further and simplify test design by condensing it into an easy to understand Activity Diagram.

Now I am going to show how to select tests from the potential tests identified in the last chapter and group them into Test Cases.

Grouping Tests into Test Cases

As I mentioned earlier, Essential Test Cases describe groups of tests based on scenarios or flows of the Use Case. To group tests you start by selecting tests.

To group tests into Essential Test Cases here is what to do.

Identify initial Test cases by grouping tests according to Use Cases.

- Start with positive tests.
- For each Use Case look at the happy path first. This can provide an initial test scenario.
- Group tests that support each alternate path in the Use Case: Those too are Test Cases.
- Test cases can also be built around partial sections of any Use Case flow.
- Next, look for negative tests in the variant table that also can be grouped by the flows of the Use Case. Create Test Cases from them.
- Then look at off-nominal conditions not covered by the above Use Case flows. Remember, these are conditions where the requirements may not be clear about what the system will do. Set these up as separate Test Cases.
- Group negative tests where the System State is not a normal operational state for a given flow.
- Next examine all the remaining tests. Some may be incorporated into existing Test Cases. Create individual Test Cases for any that are left over.

- Finally, take a look back and see what else you might imagine would be a good test but is not apparent by the table. Such as, what would happen if the power went out – twice? Or, what happens if two successive sensors report good data but BOTH were actually wrong? Think outside the box!

An Example using the process:

Here is a brief example limited to the basic flow of our example Use Case.

We first look at the positive tests of the basic flow of the Use Case and group the following variants:

Variant 1: Open Lane Request valid

Variant 3: Destination ID valid

Variant 6: Lane Selection/Package Limit valid

Variant 18: Open Gate valid

Variant 22 Gate response = gate open

This will be the Test Case *"Open a Lane Basic Flow Positive Test"*.

Once we have the positive Test Case, we group the rest of the tests based on steps in the basic flow: Destination Selection, Lane Selection, Opening Gate, and add a Test Case to cover negative tests caused by System States.

Open A Lane Basic Flow Negative Tests For *Destination Selection*

Variant 2: Open Lane Request invalid

Variant 4: Destination ID invalid format

Variant 5: Destination ID selected not in system

Open A Lane Basic Flow Negative Tests For *Lane Selection*

Variant 7: Lane Selection/Package Limit = held/valid

Variant 8: Lane Selection/Package Limit = assigned/valid

Variant 9: Lane Selection/Package Limit = invalid lane/valid

Variant 10: Lane Selection/Package Limit = no lane selected/valid

Variant 11: Lane Selection/Package Limit = valid/ limit set to 0

Open A Lane Basic Flow Negative Tests For *Opening Gate*

Variant 19:Open Gate - invalid format

Variant 20:Open Gate - wrong gate specified

Variant 21:Open Gate – no command

Variant 23:Gate Response – gate locked error

Variant 24:Gate Response – no response

Open A Lane Basic Flow Negative Tests Due To System State

Variant 25: No lanes available

Variant 26: Lane assignments to destination at limit

Variant 27: Selected gate already open

Variant 28: Dispatch system not available

Selecting Tests

I just showed how potential tests can be selected by grouping test to run as Essential Test Cases. As far as I'm concerned, that is the bulk of the selection process.

But wait, there *is* more.

I jumped right into selecting tests for Test Cases without going into the philosophy of test selection. Why? Because for an Essential Tester that stuff takes second fiddle to actually knowing how to select tests.

Remember, as an Essential Tester you understand your environment early and learn what it will take to prove the system. This includes knowing what needs to be proven and to what level of detail is needed. As part of initial planning you figured these things out.

As the project progresses and stakeholder perceptions change, the details of what needs to be tested may change. You still understand what needs to be tested because you expect change and have no problem keeping up with it.

When you follow the steps just described to identify potential tests, many of the tests to keep will become obvious as you identify them. That's because you have a clear understanding of what it will take to prove the system.

Despite my comments above, I'm going to talk a little bit in this chapter about the broader picture of selecting tests from the potential tests.

The rest of this section covers how to select tests to ensure you know how to.

In other words, how to:

- determine the essential tests that must be run,
- eliminate unnecessary tests, and
- augment the list of tests to ensure coverage of requirements, especially those that may not have been mapped to Use Cases.

Determine What Tests MUST Be Run

To determine what tests to run first identify the features important to stakeholders that must be proved. Select tests that verify those features.

The most important functionality of the system in the eyes of the stakeholders is identified during test planning. But Stakeholders change their mind. So check to make sure that the functionality identified then still holds the same importance to the stakeholders. Then identify tests that prove that functionality.

Next, identify tests that prove functionality vital to system operation. Identify functionality that must work in order for the rest of the system to work correctly.

Use corresponding requirements to help select tests to prove the important functionality.

War Story

I worked on a project that developed software to control a satellite system. The software would be responsible for starting up the system, handling communication with a ground station, and controlling functionality to perform the satellite's mission.

Although the satellite's mission was the most important aspect of the system in the eyes of the stakeholders, it was also vital that communication with the ground station and starting the system worked correctly.

In fact these two aspects could be more important. It didn't matter how well the system controlled satellite mission functionality if the satellite couldn't communicate with the ground properly or the system couldn't start up. Then, the satellite would be no more valuable than a floating brick.

On the other hand, if the mission software didn't work properly, as long as the satellite can communicate with the ground station, software can be upgraded on the ground, uploaded to the satellite, and rebooted.

continued...

So, although we wanted the whole system to work, we really needed to weight our focus towards communications and start up. So, while it may not be intuitive that the startup should be tested as much or more than the flight control software it's thinking outside the box that makes testers the heroes.

Eliminate Unnecessary Tests

Once the important functionality has been examined and initial tests selected, review the variant table of potential tests to determine:

- tests that may be dropped
- tests that are redundant

And, of course at the same time don't forget, as an Essential Tester, you don't want to do any more testing than needed to prove the system.

Drop Insignificant Tests

Some potential tests may not be significant for example, conditions covered by other tests, or tests of functionality whose failure is of little consequence to the success of the system as a whole.

I start by looking at potential tests where the system takes no action: prime candidates for dropping.

For example, look at variants 20 and 21 in the *Open A Lane* Use Case. No requirements were specified for these variants; there may be a reason. So, you find out why.

In talking to stakeholders and requirements analysts, I found out that no requirements were specified because the occurrence specified - *Package limit being entered is in an invalid format or not being entered at all* - is one they consider rare and of little importance. So, with agreement from the stakeholders that those conditions will not have to be tested these variants were dropped.

Another example. variants 12 through 15 are combinations of negative values for Operational Variables *Lane Selection* and *Package Limit*. Since the variant table already has negative tests for the individual conditions of each Operational Variable (variants 7 through 11) you don't need to test this combination of negative values. (The stakeholders agreed and those variants were dropped.)

Defining Essential Test Cases

Now that you know how to group tests into Test Cases, the next step is to build them. I am going to show you how in two parts. In the rest of this chapter I will cover defining the tests. In the next chapter I will show you how to create the test design and include it into the Test Case.

Filling In Test Cases I: The Test Definition Section

If initial Test Cases have been identified, by grouping and selecting tests as described in the previous section, the work of creating test definitions for Test Cases has already been done. It is now a matter of filling in the right information into the body of each Test Case. This information comes from the variant tables.

Remember, variant tables hold information about test preconditions (System State), test inputs (Operational Variables) and expected results - think of the variants in the variant table as mini Test Cases.

I include a Test Case template in Appendix C. For now I will focus on the definition portion.

In the body of the Test Case define what is being tested with the following.

Name: identifies the Test Case. Give the Test Case a name related to the type of test and the Use Case and flow it is related to.

Description: what the Test Case will verify and a general description of what takes place during the test.

Requirements Covered: optional depending on the needs of the testing team. It may serve as a reference tying the Test Case to requirements. But if the project is tracing requirements to Test Cases it would be redundant.

Preconditions: can be composed from system state information in the variant table.

Input: should come straight from the Operational Variables for the variants being covered.

Expected Results: should come from the expected results described for the covered test variants

Test Case Example 1:

The following is a description of the test definition portion of a test case.

Name: Open a Lane Basic flow Positive Test

Description:

This Test Case validates the system can properly respond to inputs into the system under normal conditions described in the basic flow of the Open a Lane Use Case. Multiple positive tests are combined to verify system outcome throughout the steps of the basic flow.

The following conditions will be tested by this Test Case:

An Open Lane Request is valid (Variant 1)

An existing Destination ID is entered in a valid format (Variant 3)

Valid Lane Selection and Package Limit are inputted into the system (Variant 6)

A valid Open Gate command is received by the system (Variant 18)

A Gate response of "gate open" is received by the system in response to a request to open a gate (Variant 22)

Requirements covered

SRS 2: The system shall display lanes assigned to a destination upon request.

The system shall display available lanes upon request.

The system shall identify that a lane is available if it is not currently assigned to a lane and is not being held for future use

SRS 3: The system shall allow only available lanes to be assigned to a destination. (Partially tested)

SRS 5: The system shall provide conveyor operators with the capability of associating available lanes to destinations.

SRS 6: The system shall provide conveyor operators with the capability of opening a physical lane gate on request.

SRS 7: The system shall designate a gate as "Opened" when the corresponding physical gate is opened.

SRS 9: The system shall only open a physical gate corresponding to a gate that is assigned. (partially tested)

SRS 12: The system shall store gate/destination assignment once an assigned gate is determined to be "Open".

SRS 13: The system shall send gate/destination assignment to the dispatch system when a gate is determined to be assigned and open.

SRS 19: The system shall accept and recognize a value associated with a lane/destination assignment representing the maximum amount of packages that may be diverted to the lane.

Preconditions

- The system is operational and lanes are available for assignment

Test Inputs

Open Lane Request: A valid request to initiate activities to assign a lane to a destination and physically open the corresponding lane.

Destination ID: A valid identifier for the destination the Conveyor Operator intends to assign a lane to.

Lane Selection: A valid selection representing the lane intended to be assigned to a destination. This value is entered in conjunction with Package Limit.

Package Limit: A valid numeric value limiting the number of packages that can be diverted to an assigned lane.

Open Gate: A valid request by Conveyor Operator to coordinate activities to physically open a gate on the conveyor associated with an assigned lane.

Gate Response: A message received from the Divert Lane Control system indicating a gate has been successfully opened.

Expected Test Results

- The system prompts for a destination upon receiving a valid Open Lane Request.
- The system displays lanes currently assigned to the requested destination and the lanes currently available in response to a valid Destination ID.
- The system assigns the lane, records the Package Limit, and prompts to open the gate on the conveyor associated with the lane. This is in response to a valid lane selection and Package ID.
- The system responds to a valid Open Gate command by sending a request to the divert lane control.
- In response to a Gate Response indicating the gate has been opened, the system:
- Stores the gate and destination information
- Sends the Dispatch System with the lane and destination assignment information indicating packages can be assigned to the lane.
- Notifies the Conveyor Operator

Comments On This Example

Here is the important stuff from the above example.

The Description mentions the flow being tested. This is a reference to the portion of the Use Case being tested. I also listed functionality being tested. I got that from the variants we selected for this Test Case.

In the Requirements Covered section I identified the functional requirements the Use Case flow being tested. Like I mentioned before, this is optional. I also placed the text of each addressed requirement in the section. Normally references are good enough. Also, I have some of the requirements listed as partially tested. This says that other Test Cases will have to cover aspects missed by this Test Case. Requirements are determined to be partially tested based on analysis.

What I have just given you constitutes the test definition portion of the Test Case. Next you add the test design part.

This would be the finish for a traditional Test Case. Except for Environment. I consider Environment as the start of Design. Next chapter!

Chapter 16

Adding Test Design To Your Test Case

In the last chapter, I introduced a very important part of Essential Testing - using Test Cases to document both 'test definition', their traditional role – and Test Design. I spent most of the last chapter talking about defining tests, but haven't covered test design.

In this chapter, I'll add in the Test Design elements - Environment and Procedure – that you will use to complete an Essential Test Case.

As I mentioned before, David DeWitt and I came up with a way of designing tests as we defined them – combine definition and design in the Test Cases!

I like including test design with test definition because then everything you need to create your test is in one place. In the first part of the Test Case you have all the information about what you are testing, what inputs will be used in the test, and the expected results. The design part (the procedure) shows how the test process will work using all the ingredients of the Test Case to perform the test. A single Test Case document can be handed over to a test builder with enough information to build the test.

However, if you don't feel comfortable including your test

design in the body of your Test Cases, keep them separate. It won't be Essential, though.

First, I'll discuss test environment. Then I'll discuss describing how tests will be performed in the form of Procedures. This is the order that design is described: first understand the test environment, and then define the procedure to get the test done.

Test Environment

The test environment is composed of the hardware and software the tests will run on. The environment must be defined before you can define how tests will be run.

Fill in the Test Environment section by including any hardware and software items that will be used to test. First identify hardware. Hardware items include computers the software under test will run on, devices that will monitor test result outputs (oscilloscopes), hardware simulation software will run on, and devices that interact with the software under test.

Software items include the software under test, simulation software, test monitoring software, software used to interpret results, and operating systems.

When filling in this section sketch out a scenario of the activities involved in testing. This is a precursor to designing the test with procedures. The actual flow will come later. Think about the software and hardware required to perform the activities required to run the test defined so far in the Test Case. Look at all activities including test set up, running the test, and evaluating results. For each activity list the hardware and software available to use for testing. Include all components you can think of in the initial pass. List the environment components in the Test Environment section of the Test Case.

An Example of Test Environment

In the example for the Test Case for *Open a Lane Basic Flow Positive Test,* the first thing to do is understand how the test environment can be set up. Enter this information in the Environmental Needs section of the Test Case. The focus is on the software and hardware that will enable the test to be performed. This is not a wish list. This is based on what is practical.

We know we'll use

- an automated GUI testing tool that is readily available to automate interaction with the system under test.
- a conveyor simulator created in-house that runs on a PC card plugged into a conveyor back panel that also holds the PC card the system under test runs on. Devices, including lane gates, can be configured into the simulator for example to simulate the opening of a gate.
- an instance of the Dispatch system used to verify that the system under test sends proper lane assignment information to the dispatch system.

For the example I entered this information into the Environmental Needs section of the Test Case as follows.

Environmental Needs

Hardware

- Two PC Pentium 4 cards inserted into slots one and two of a back plane configured for a conveyor system.
- A conveyor back plane power supply
- A display monitor and keyboard connected to the PC card in slot 1.
- A display monitor and keyboard connected to the PC card in slot 2.

- PC system with monitor to be used for the automated testing software.

Software

- Automated GUI testing software installed on the PC system slot 1
- System Under Test installed on PC card in slot 1
- Conveyor simulator software installed on PC card in slot 2
- Instance of Dispatch system running on PC system slot 1

Test Participants

Test participants are part of the test environment: anything or anyone participating in the test. Participants can include testers, simulators, test tools, and the System Under Test. Anything that does something – including all activities from test set up through test evaluation – is a candidate.

Test Participants can be gleaned from the test environment defined for the test. In our example, Tester is an obvious Test Participant. The tester will set up the test, initiate it, and evaluate it. The System Under Test is another obvious participant. It will respond to the tests. Without it there is no point in testing. Others that may be less obvious now include the conveyor simulator, the automated GUI tester, and the Dispatch system. These will become apparent as the design progresses.

Procedures: How A Test Will Be Performed

How a test will be performed – the design - doesn't need an elaborate description; diagrams are enough. These will be placed in the Procedure section of the Test Case.

I prefer using UML Activity Diagrams to show what happens in a test and who the participants are. You don't have to use Activity Diagrams, but I recommend them. They are easy to understand and combine test flow with responsibilities of test participants.

Activity Diagrams For Testers

Activity Diagrams are the UML version of a flowchart. They show process flow, and are typically used to model business process flows.

I use them to show the flow of a test and the test participant responsible for any given test activity.

I'll use the diagram, (figure 16-1), as an example of an Activity Diagram describing the generic activities involved in performing a test.

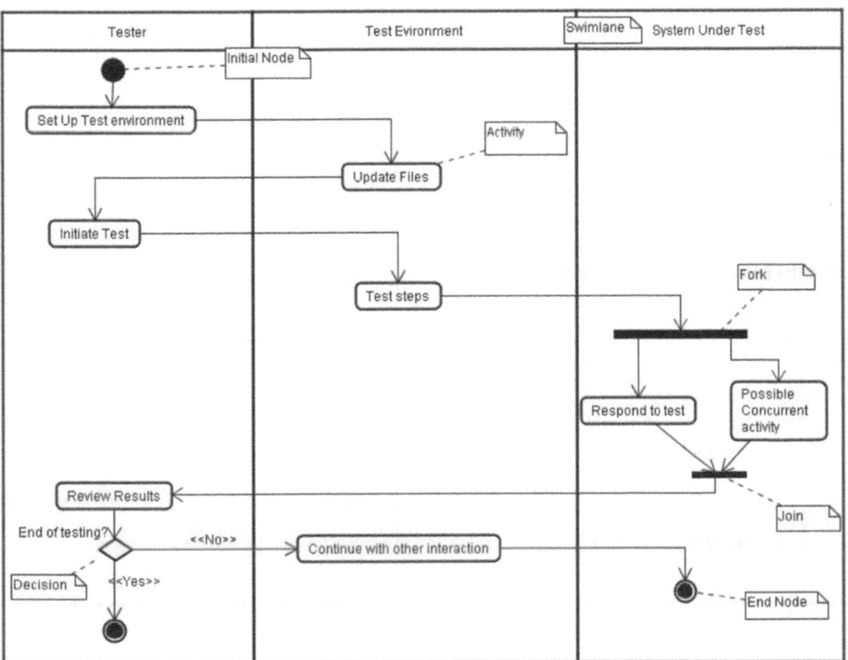

Figure 16-1: Example of an Activity Diagram for a generic test

The following table explains the diagram components.

	Initial node	The start of the process.
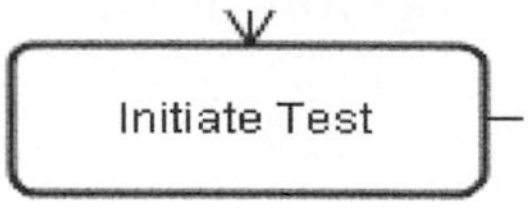 Initiate Test	**Activity**	Activities can be manual or automated. For example, a manual activity would be *Review Results Performed By A Tester,* while an automated activity would be *Update Files Performed By The System.*
	Swimlane	Swimlanes partition the workflow according to who or what is responsible for performing individual activities. For testing, the swimlanes will represent test participants. My example in figure 19-1 is organized into three partitions indicating which activates will be handled by the *Tester, Test Environment, or System.* This can also help with test setup and planning. Activities partitioned to a tester are most likely manual activities, while activities performed by the Environment will be automated.
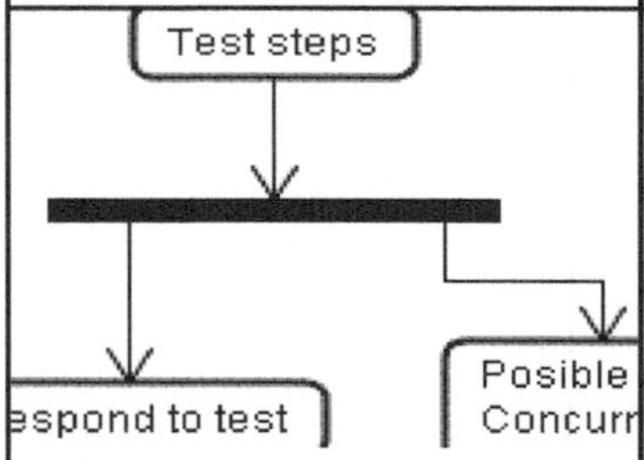 Test steps espond to test Posible Concurr	**Fork:**	Used to manage parallel activities in the model, that is, multiple activities that can be performed concurrently right after a preceding individual activity.
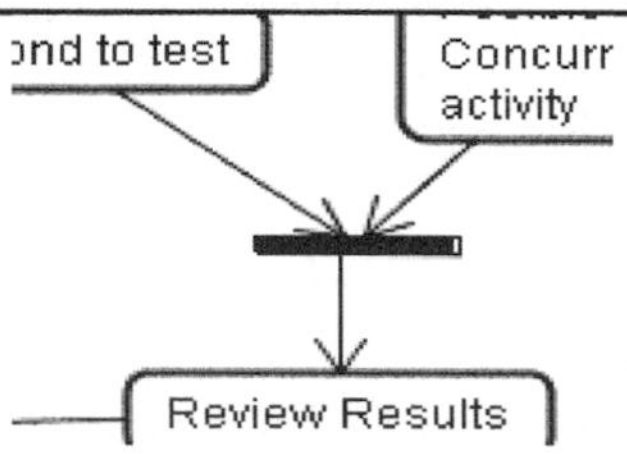 ond to test Concurr activity Review Results	**Join:**	Shows the convergence of parallel activities as they finish. All parallel activities that happen between a fork and join have to finish for the join to be considered complete.
	**Activity final node.**	Ending point of the process. An activity diagram can have more that one activity final nodes

Table 16-1 Activity Diagram Components

Describing the Test With An Activity Diagram

First review the Test Environment section of the Test Case to determine the test participants that will be responsible for performing specific test activities – the 'players' in each test scenario.

There's an informal pattern here.

I usually start with a Tester, a Test environment, and the System (the system under test). You may need to identify other players, such as emulators or external systems. All of these will end up represented by swimlanes in the Test Case Activity Diagram.

Then take a look at the definition portion of the Test Case and decide what activities will be needed to set up, perform, and analyze results for the test it describes. Finally associate activities with the test participants.

The first activities will identify test set up followed by the actual test and finally test wrap up and analysis.

Most of the time, the Tester will be responsible for setting up the test environment including activities such as:

- running a program to restore files
- running other tests to get the system in the proper state
- Manually setting up files that must be in place to run tests, or system parameters

Test execution activities can include:

- test initiation
- simulation of inputs
- manual input of data
- response by the system under test

Wrap up and analysis activities can include:

- storing results
- processing test result data
- automated analysis of results
- manual analysis of results

Identify individual steps required to test as specific activities. Attach notes to activities to describe additional test details as necessary.

Activities will be placed in the swimlanes of the test participants performing the activities.

The value of an Activity Diagram is Efficient Communication. The Tester creating the test can use the diagram along with the rest of the Test Case to understand how to build the test.

An Example Of An Activity Diagram For a Test Case

I will now walk through the creation of an Activity Diagram continuing with the example for the Open a Lane Basic Flow Positive Test:

- I first identify test participants by looking at the Test Environment section of the Test Case I filled in the last example. I know there will be an automated GUI testing tool as part of the test environment, the system under test, a conveyor simulator, and a Dispatch system.
- There will also be a Tester. I set up the initial Activity Diagram partitioning those participants into swimlanes.
- After reviewing the entire Test Case created so far I identify activities and create the Activity Diagram for the Test Case shown in figure 16-2 below.
- Once the Activity Diagram is complete it is placed in the Test Procedures section of the Test Case.

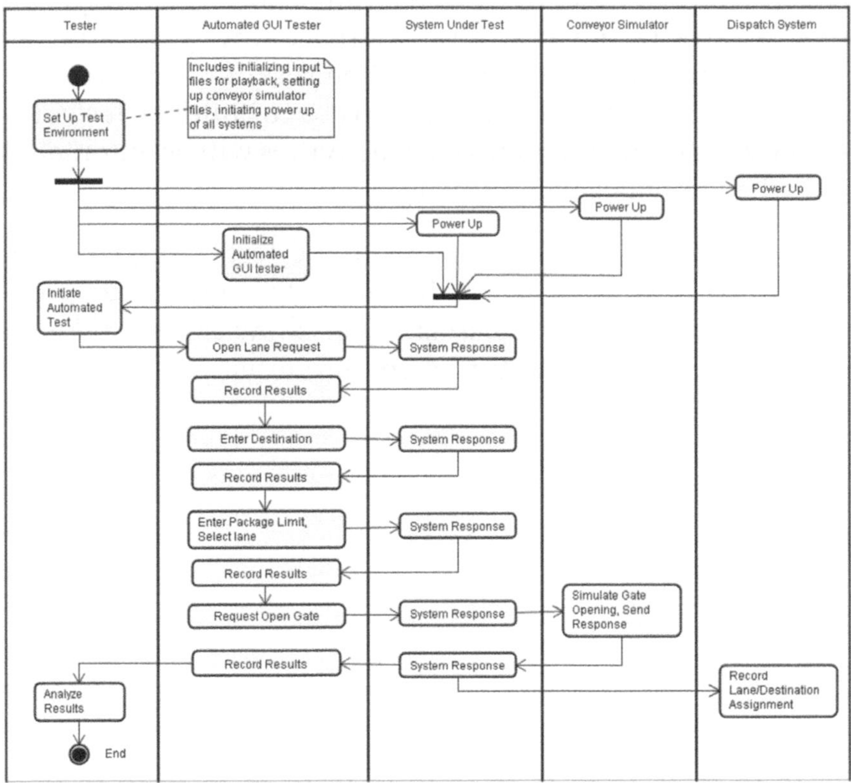

Figure 16-2 Example of Activity Diagram for 1 Open a Lane Basic Flow Positive Test Test Case

The flow of the test is shown beginning with the tester setting up the test environment and then initiating the test. Most of the activities after that take place between the Automated GUI Test tool and the system under test. For each activity initiated by the automated test tool, the system under test responds. I don't specify how the system responds, because I won't know the actual response until the test takes place. I can link notes to the system responses and specify expected results.

Looking at the rest of the Activity Diagram you can see what the simulator and Dispatch system do. The last activity of analyze results belongs to the tester, and after that the process ends.

What I like about the Activity Diagram is that you can quickly get a feel for where activities take place throughout the test flow. This information along with the rest of the information in the Test Case should be enough to use to build the tests. The Activity Diagram illustrates what activities will be automated, and what activities will be manual.

Now that design is incorporated into the Test Cases, you have everything you need to create the tests required to prove the system. In the next chapter I will show how to take the Essential Test Cases and turn them into tests.

Chapter 17

Creating Tests

Once design information is incorporated into Test Cases, there is enough information to create the corresponding tests.

In this section I will discuss first looking for existing tests that may be used to create new tests from to save time and energy. Next I will show you how to create detailed test instructions in the form of Test Procedures.

Harvesting Tests

The next thing to do is see if there are any existing tests similar to the ones we are going to build: borrow them. I call that test harvesting, others call it stealing.

Harvesting tests consists of looking for tests that may be reused either as is or with modifications. The motive is to help speed up test development. Tests previously created for a similar product or a previous version of the system to be tested may be ripe for harvesting.

War Story

I once worked on a large project where we were tasked with doing black box testing for a particular product. There was another test team doing white box testing on the same product using the same test environment and the same scripting language. We were able to schedule the test creation work of the two groups to reduce redundancy. The white box testers harvested test the black box testers created and vice-versa. Of course both groups had to modify tests to meet their own specific needs, but each group was able to save time by harvesting from the other.

When harvesting tests make sure they are worth harvesting. If the tests are in poor shape or don't fit well with the existing test suite, it may be better to build from scratch. Still, it doesn't hurt to take a look first.

To harvest tests review Test Cases against lists and documentation on existing tests that may be of interest. When potential tests are found, look deeper into corresponding Test Cases, Test Procedures, and test scripts. Try to get a feel for the magnitude of changes that will be required if the test is harvested. As part of harvesting, review requirements that the harvested test will cover. Once the test is deemed harvestable, document it for the test creators.

Creating Test Procedures

After harvesting, create Test Procedures and corresponding tests.

Test Procedures describe the details of the activities a tester must perform to execute tests described in a Test Case. These are instructions the testers use to conduct tests.

Use Activity Diagrams to Create Test Procedures

Test creation depends on the test environment available and the types of testing planned, including the level of involvement of testing personnel. You get this information from the Activity Diagrams in the Test Case.

Start by determining what combination of manual and automated testing is needed.

- Manual tests are tests with a high degree of tester interaction. Many of the tests are scripted in step-by-step documents that a tester must follow. Often, testing takes place in front of a User Interface that resembles the final product such as a website. In other cases manual testing may take place with a user interface into a simulator where the tester supplies inputs to the simulator which converts the information into messages to the System Under Test.
- In automated tests the tester usually sets up the test environment and initiates a set of tests that bypass most tester interaction. In some cases portions of the analysis of test results may be automated as well.

In many cases tests will be composed of a combination of manual and automated events.

Up until now I have encouraged you to use as few artifacts as possible and employ as little rigor as possible to successfully test the system. In the case of Test Procedures, I want to stress that you need to get these right. Accuracy in testing is vital to having confidence in the tests, so it is critical that the test instructions are understandable and correct.

Test Procedure Components

I included a Test Procedure template in Appendix C. The main components that make it up are:

- What the procedure is for

- Procedure specific files
- Test set up
- Test Procedure steps
- Test evaluation instructions

The first section identifies the Test Case the procedure is for. Multiple procedures may be required to cover a Test Case

The next section, Procedure specific files, identifies parameter files and databases required for the test. It also includes vales for the files and databases and specific instructions for setting them up.

The Test set up section describes step-by-step instructions for setting up the tests. This includes turning on hardware, hooking up test monitoring devices, and initializing programs.

Test Procedure steps identify the steps that must be followed to run the tests. For automated tests they describe the interaction between the tester and the test environment required to run the tests. For manual tests, steps describe the interaction between tester and test interface including values to enter and expected results. I like to use a table to describe test steps and include expected results where appropriate. I like to identify the requirements each step tests and if the requirement is completely or partially tested.

The Test Evaluation section provides instructions for evaluating the test including running programs that process raw data. This section may not be necessary for some manual tests where evaluation can take place as the procedure steps are followed.

To create tests I find that it helps to take a two pass process.

The First Pass

In the first pass review the Activity Diagram in the Test Case. This should provide a good illustration of the flow of events that must take place to fulfill the test. It will also give an understanding of how the tests are to be written for each test participant. There may be multiple Activity Diagrams for a Test Case indicating multiple Test Procedures.

For each procedure determine the order of tests that will take place and sketch out the steps to be performed within the test environment. Then identify inputs and their data values:

- For manual tests this may take the form of a written list.
- For automated tests this may require identifying test files and formats.

Then identify test evaluation activities, file locations, observation activities, and analysis tools. Also identify any automated analysis.

Next review tests slated for harvesting and determine how they fit into the tests being created. For tests being harvested, fill in the details in the Test Procedures with harvested information where appropriate.

The Final Pass

In the final pass start by identifying any automated tests that need to be written.

Then for manual tests, build the appropriate written steps for the tester to follow. Include them in the body of the procedure. Identify any interactions with simulation software including activities to build input files. At this point your procedure should be filled in.

To finish, create automated tests that may be necessary and unit test them. Once all tests related to a Test Procedure have been built, follow the Test Procedure to test the tests and debug them. Make any changes to the Test Procedures as needed.

As part of creating tests, the Test Procedure is pivotal. As the instruction set the tester will follow, it ties the tests together. Here is an example.

A Test Procedure Example for the Open Lane Basic Flow Positive Test Test Case

Test Procedures for Open a Lane Basic Flow Positive Test

ID: TP 1

Procedure Specific Files

Dispatch System Output log file: This file contains a log of messages received from the system under test. This file is automatically initialized when the application Dispatch Application is run. No set up is required.

Conveyor Simulator parameter table: This file contains parameters to simulate an active conveyor system. It holds information that describes lane assignments the simulated system will be initialized to and the packages that will be simulated as moving through the simulated conveyor system.

File Format: As description of file format can be found in document ConveyorSimulatorParameterFile.doc.

File Parameters: Parameter specifics for this file are described in the document called SimulatorSetUpTP1

File location name: ConveyorSetUpTP1

File location: PC2 folder location c:\Simulator

Set Up: prior to testing access PC2 and copy file ConveyorSetUpTP1 from c:\simulatorSetUpFiles to c:\Simulator

Automated GUI Test Parameter file: This holds information that is used to drive the automated test for the test described in this Test Procedure. This is a system file crated automatically using the GUI testing tool. It doesn't need to be loaded for this test.

Test Environment Set Up

Test environment setup steps are as follows:

- Turn on Monitor for PC1 (labeled)
- Turn on Monitor for PC2
- Turn on power (black button) for the Conveyor Box (labeled "Conveyor System Box").
- Windows system will be displayed in monitor for PC1.
- Windows System will be displayed in monitor for PC2.
- Select Conveyor Simulator Icon on PC2 using the arrows on the keypad labeled (PC2)
- The monitor for PC Two will display message that the conveyor is running
- Select the Dispatch System on PC1 using the arrows on the keypad labeled (PC1)
- The monitor for PC1 will display message indicating the Dispatch System is running.
- Select the System Under Test (SUT) icon on PC1 using the arrows on the keypad labeled (PC1)
- The monitor for PC1 will display message indicating SUT is running. The Window for Conveyor Monitoring is displayed.
- Select the GUI Tester Icon on PC1.
- The GUI Test window will open and list automated tests available to perform

Test Procedure Steps

Step#	TEST Step	EXPECTED RESULT	Pass/ Fail	Req	Comments
1	Bring up the GUI Test window on PC1				
2	Select Open Lane BF TC1 form the list of available tests to run				
3	Select Run Test (button)	The test should run to completion and display "Test Complete". Log file is stored as OpenLaneBFTC1 with a date/time			
4	Copy the log file named OpenLaneBFTC1 from c:\GUI Test\Log to c:\ Test Results as file name "OpenLaneBFTC1(date/ time)".				

Test Evaluation Instructions

Display the log file for the test (file "OpenLaneBFTC1(date/ time)". View the file and check the step name and corresponding results identified in the table below. For each test mark pass or fail.

Test Step Name	Expected Results	Pass/Fail
Request Open a Lane	Open Lane window Displayed showing a list of destination that may be selected Including DST1, DST2, DST3with list of available lanes.	
Destination 2 Selected	Destination2 is displayed showing Lanes 2 and 3 assigned to DST2 and Lanes 6, 7, and 8 available.	

Test Step Name	Expected Results	Pass/Fail
Lane 7 selected for Destination 2, Package limit = 100.	Lane 7 assignment to Destination 2 is displayed	
	Prompt for Open a Lane	
Request Open Gate 7	Response displayed that gate for lane 7 is open	

Check the Conveyor Simulator log file and confirm that Gate for lane 7 was opened and message sent to SUT.

Check log file for Dispatch System and verify message received from SUT that Lane 7 was assigned to Destination 2.

The above example shows the Test Procedure to positive test the happy path of the Open Lane Use Case. The information in the procedure should be detailed enough to set up, run, and evaluate the tests.

As I created the Test Procedure, I continually used the Test Case and corresponding Use Case it describes tests for.

When filling in the Procedure Specific Files section, I referred to the Test Environment section of the Test Case. I could put the file formats here if I chose to. For clarity, I refer to those details described in other supporting documents.

For the Test Environment Set Up section, I relied on both the Test Environment section and the Activity Diagram in the Test Case. With that information and knowledge of the test environment components, I was able to create the steps required to bring the system up in a state ready to run tests.

In the Test Procedure Steps section I describe the steps the tester must take to run the tests. In this case, the test is automated so I only have to describe how to initiate the test and perform house cleaning once the test is run. I don't use all the columns in the table. If I were describing a manual test there would be more information listed. In this case the detailed information related to the expected results go into the Test Evaluation Instruction section. I have an example of a Test Procedure for a manual test in Appendix B.

To fill in the Test Evaluation Instructions section I rely heavily on the Use Case, and the Test Definition and Activity Diagram in the Test Case The Activity Diagram shows the steps taken by the participants including automated test components. The Use Case gives more detail about the sequence of events, and the test definition describes inputs and expected results. You can see how the same information would be needed to build the automated tests into the GUI Tester. I created a simple table to be used to evaluate results generated by the GUI Tester.

Conclusion

I have just covered how to build tests using the test design and created Test Procedures to describe how to run those tests. Once tests are created and instructions to run them are in place, the next step is to run the tests. That is the topic of the next chapter.

Chapter 18

Executing Tests

We execute tests to find defects and report on them. If all the activities took place described in the previous chapters to plan, identify and select the right tests, build the tests and create detailed instructions on how to run and evaluate results, executing the tests should be mostly strait forward.

In order to test, the following are needed:

- The application to test
- The environment to test it in
- Tests to run
- Criteria to evaluate them
- Instructions on how to test

In recent chapters I described how to define the test environment, design and create the tests, define expected results in the Test Cases, and create test instructions in the form of Test Procedures. You have control of those artifacts so don't worry about them. In fact, if you do everything I said an Essential Tester does, executing the tests is the easy part of testing.

The only thing listed above that you don't have complete control over is the application to test. And by being proactive, you help the entire project team produce a decent application.

Still, problems will arise.

Execution Problems and Their Solution

As I mentioned at the beginning of the chapter, if everything has gone as planned, then testing should be mostly straight forward - mostly strait forward because we don't test in perfect environments.

In this section I talk about dealing with less than optimal circumstances that may face the tester at execution time.

DOA Deliveries

Most testers have been in situations when they were given lousy deliverable to test against. In some cases the testing group receives a delivery that doesn't run at all, or has too many major problems to be able to test at all.

The typical industry answer I found while researching for this book is to identify and report all visible defects that are holding up tests and notify management since the product delivered indicates there are problems with the development process.

That is one solution, and may even be the best response in some cases. Hopefully, deeper problems with development will have been caught earlier through constant communication. As the product is being developed, it shouldn't be too hard for Essential Testers to get a feel for whether requirements have stabilized and if development is based on the requirements.

Essentially, it is best to address problems when you first suspect them rather than waiting until test execution.

The first thing to do when a product isn't testable is to go talk to the developers and find out more information. I have seen people write defects on products that seem to not work only to find out the test environment wasn't configured properly. That doesn't bode well for working relationships. The people handing over a product don't want to hand over something that doesn't work any more than a tester wants to receive it. It may be best to hold off on the defects for a bit and allow the developers a little flexibility at first. You don't want to affect schedules, but working with developers and integrators to get a testable product goes a long way, and you don't want to scare the stakeholders if it isn't warranted.

War Story

I worked on one iterative development project where we executed functional tests and reported on them for each iteration application build. Stakeholders had full visibility to defects. The first iteration was a disaster. We got a build that had major defects that caused some delays but also caused concern from the stakeholders that things weren't going well. We worked with the developers and came up with a plan for future iterations where we would have two levels of functional testing. The first would be an informal test where the developers would deliver the product a couple of days prior to the official start of testing for an iteration. We would sit with the developers and run our planned tests as best we could while identifying but not officially recording defects. That way, the developers were aware of potentially embarrassing problems before they actually got recorded. The result was a product that was more reliable when the official functional tests were performed and a decent working relationship between development and test.

Changing Stakeholder Perception

As the product is tested and the stakeholder sees features come to life, the importance of the features may change. This may require slight changes in presentation strategies or even the level of testing. This can also cause requirements to change late in the game. Often this is a project management issue but testing personnel may also help deal with this type of situation. By keeping a constant rapport with the stakeholders, testers can position themselves to adjust quickly to perception changes. Many times the solution is nothing more than an additional report or slight changes in existing tests.

Timing of Tests

Timing tests, determining when to run them, can be a source of execution problems. Test timing depends on the project process. Traditionally, most testing to prove the system is done against delivered code. For projects employing Agile methodologies, this means testing early and often since code delivery is early and often. In an agile environment timing isn't even a consideration.

For iterative development most tests will be executed towards the end of each iteration.

For waterfall methodologies, test execution takes place towards the end of the project as releases of functionality occur. Test timing would have been taken into account when doing the initial planning. Most likely the initial plan wasn't accurate. Changes to the environment, in release strategies, in what the stakeholders need to see, and project delays will cause a plan to be inaccurate. As Essential Testers, make adjustments from the original plan as changes happen, but remember evaluate the impact of those adjustments before entering into test execution. Some last minute tweaking may be in order.

Special Considerations at Test Execution Time

Executing Regression Tests

Regression testing is done to ensure that something that was previously working still works. It doesn't focus on new functionality, but on functionality that was previously delivered and tested. As new functionality is added to a product tests are run to make sure nothing previously delivered got broken. Defects of this type include:

- existing uncaught defects that show up with the integration of new code
- defects previously fixed that reappear in the new release
- defects on previous functionality introduced as part of the creation of new functionality.

Regression tests are generally identified from previously run tests. Common ways to regression test include performing all previously run tests, focusing on the reemergence of previously found bugs, and running a subset of previously run tests focusing on critical functionality.

Rerunning all previously run tests on a product can be time consuming, especially when manual tests are involved. When most of the tests are automated, it may be possible to run all test without human intervention. An option is to start regression tests at the end of a day, let them run overnight, and analyze results in the morning.

Running regression tests to see if previously fixed bugs have reemerged is another method of regression testing. A reason for focusing on previously fixed bugs is because defects often have a way of showing up in code after they have been fixed. Reasons for this include improper or poor version control, fragile code, or redesigning existing features introduces past mistakes. This method can be useful but it focuses on past problems. Testers must still worry that either previously undiscovered bugs haven't emerged or new critical defects haven't been created.

Another way of regression testing is to use a subset of previously run tests to focus on critical functionality. This reduces the effort of running and analyzing all previously run tests by only executing what is deemed critical. This allows testers to focus on what the stakeholder considers important as well as critical functionality required to run the new tests and potential reemerging defects.

Executing Manual and Automatic Tests

The effort involved in testing manually is not always greater than the effort to execute automated tests. Complexity of the test environments, the test preparation effort, and the effort to analyze results affect the testing effort. Different tester skills may be required for the two types of tests. In the case of manual testing, testers may have to emulate end user behavior. In the case of automated testing, testers may have to be more technical savvy. More training may be required for testers performing automated testing.

Even in executing tests we must be flexible. We may have planned for and created automated tests for a given feature. As you test you may find the test is not adequate and the test must either be modified or supplement with another test.

Recording and Reporting Test Results

Test Recording

Defects are recorded to notify the development team of things that need to be fixed and help them prioritize those fixes. Defect recording also serves the purpose of notifying management and the stakeholders of progress. As tests are evaluated pass/fail guidelines are used to determine defects. Those defects are then evaluated against broader project or organization criteria to determine the severity of the defect. Usually the most severe defects will cause the system to crash or not allow further testing of the product to continue, while the least severe have minimal noticeable effects on the product. Severity standards should be put in place during test planning.

Defects are recorded and reported on. The repository for defects depends on the method of recording. There are many tools available for defect tracking. What is used depends on the needs of the project and benefit provided.

When a bug is detected take time to analyze the problem when recording the defect. When it comes to finding defects there is a fine line between being thorough, and being zealous. The key is to make informed decisions and often knowing the expected results is not enough.

I have worked on projects where testers with good intentions find all kinds of defects only to find out later on that a large percentage of them are determined to not be defects. Things like this lead to finger pointing and animosity between tester and others on the project. These types of problems can be minimized through communication with stakeholder, developers, and other project members.

Test Reporting

Test reporting is used to report aspects of testing results that are important to the project. Reporting is done to help show progress as well as help identify issues to be addressed by the project. Reports depend on the target audience. Reports can be generated to show defect status, severity, resolution rates, time to resolve defects, and more. Often the test group will determine the types of reports to produce in the planning process with help from other project roles such as project management, developers, and stakeholders.

Test reporting should point out testing shortcomings as well as others. Reporting on erroneously identified defects and severity is an example.

As testing takes place, coverage analysis may also take place as required. Coverage analysis measures the amount of code covered by tests being executed. Often this includes instrumenting code to run with a code coverage tool that identifies coverage as tests are run. It also includes gathering the proper information and reporting on it. Coverage analysis often depends on project expectations. Coverage level requirements are usually set up as part of the planning process.

Knowing When to Stop Testing

A friend of mine who paints pictures told me that a painting is never finished; you just have to find an interesting place to stop. While I don't want to compare testing to art, the same holds true with knowing when testing is complete. Many software applications are so complex that complete testing is out of the question. The "interesting place to stop" for testing, is mostly in the eyes of the stakeholders. We base most of our testing on what is acceptable to the stakeholders and balance that with our understanding of what makes up a quality system. Acceptable stopping points often are a combination of reducing defects below an agreed to level and reaching certain levels of test coverage.

Chapter 19

Essential Traceability

Traceability is something that happens throughout a project, usually as early as requirements gathering. Although I mention traceability in other parts of the book, it is significant enough to merit its own section. Now that I have covered the testing process I must cover traceability in more detail.

From a testing perspective, traceability and test coverage go hand in hand. The right level of test coverage can be shown through traceability.

Way back in Chapter 2, I provided definitions for traceability and coverage:

- Traceability is tracing requirements up to features or stakeholder needs, or down to design, code, and tests. For testing purposes you have to be able to trace requirements to tests in order to prove that requirements are covered by tests - one purpose of traceability is to help verify that all requirements are implemented and that the application only implemented the requirements.

- Coverage has two meanings. The first is requirements coverage by tests - are there sufficient tests to cover requirements to the level of detail needed to prove the System? The other is code coverage. This measures the source code covered by tests.

Success in achieving the right level of test coverage can only be demonstrated by means of your traceability documentation.

But traceability supports many other needs in a project. I'll deal with some of these later.

Traceability

Tracing Artifacts

Here are typical artifacts and traceability relationships found on a standard project (see Figure 19-1).

- stakeholder needs include features of the system, general system architecture, and other documents that describe the system in the view of the stakeholders. In validating requirements it is often necessary to trace requirements to the stakeholder needs in order to show that requirements communicate these needs properly and completely as the basis for building the system.
- requirements can include traditional functional and non-functional requirements as well as Use Cases. And, as I've stressed before, Use Cases may not be the actual requirements but a means of grouping them. This means that traditional functional and non-functional requirements can trace to Use Case.
- Also traceability can be between requirements when they are connected. For example, non-functional requirements may need to be traced to functional requirements when they support functionality specified, making it easier to demonstrate both requirements are covered.
- Design elements. Requirements can trace to the design. The design must be consistent with the requirements, so it follows that the requirements trace to the design. Design elements to be traced to can include

implementation specific textual specifications and models. such as sequence diagrams, class specifications and operation definitions.

- Code is usually written from a good design, but sometimes there is enough information in the requirements to write code directly. So code can trace from both requirements and design artifacts. Tracing code to requirements and tests is also required in safety critical systems.

- Test artifacts can trace to all the other major artifacts, but the key for testing is tracing to requirements.

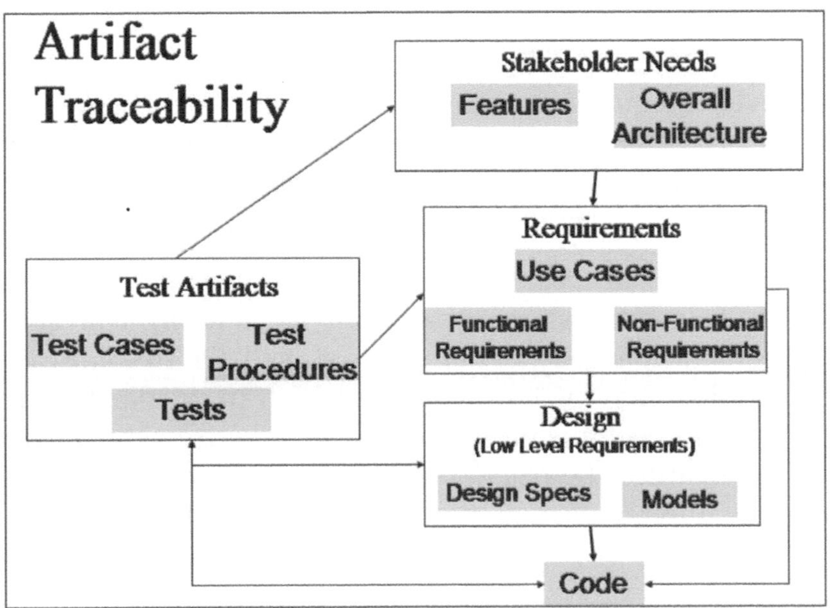

Figure 19-1 Artifact Traceability

Coverage

Test coverage is all about having enough tests to sufficiently demonstrate that the system meets specifications as perceived by the stakeholders.

The focus of test coverage is usually between the tests and the requirements – do the tests cover all the requirements identified? We want to be able to prove the requirements were satisfied. While this is an important aspect of coverage, your coverage strategy may need to be deeper than that. The amount of coverage depends on what needs to be proven to the stakeholders.

You may also need to demonstrate test coverage of design elements and code.

Requirements Coverage

The level of requirements coverage by tests depends, as usual, on the project and what is feasible. Many times stakeholders are okay with less than 100% coverage, and many times 100% coverage isn't always feasible.

For example, there may be many outcomes described by requirements where it is only feasible to test some requirements partially, or perhaps not at all. Or, In some cases stakeholders may be less concerned with particular features and may not feel it is important that all requirements related to those features be tested. And, of course, where time is a factor, requirements may have to be prioritized.

Design Coverage

Sometimes certain aspects of the design must be proven, so tests may trace to portions of the design. In such cases tests may be written specifically to prove the design, or existing tests that provide coverage of requirements may be used for the same purpose. For safety critical systems, it must be shown that the design is in line with requirements and safety issues, and that all aspects of the design have been tested sufficiently.

Code Coverage

In most projects it is good enough to show requirements coverage and some design coverage. If the system performs to the specifications of the requirements and to the constraints of the design, then the code must be implemented correctly.

In regulated industries such as avionics, the stakeholders' needs for safety may drive proving test coverage of code. The regulating body (a stakeholder) will want to see that you can point to code that implements specific requirements. They will also want to see that as tests are executed, code related to the requirements being tested is executed as well.

Showing Coverage via Traces

There are many means of showing test coverage but I only want to talk about the traceability matrix. It is the most effective means I have found.

The traceability matrix is a table depicting links between one artifact type such as requirements, to another set such as tests.

Figure 19-2 shows a very simple traceability matrix. This particular matrix shows the link between functional requirements (FR) and Test Cases (TC). In this example each requirement reference in the left most column and Test Case references are identified across the top of the table. In this example there are a total of 14 requirements and 5 Test Cases to support test those requirements. For this table, an "X" identifies a link between a requirement and a Test Case indicating coverage of a requirement by a Test Case. In this example there is full coverage of requirements by Test Cases with some requirements being tested by multiple Test Cases.

For this example I only used a spreadsheet to show traceability. This is a traceability matrix in its simplest form and can be cumbersome to maintain when there are lots of "things" to trace. Requirements management tools may work better for large projects. Most requirements management tools worth their memory space provide traceability matrix displays.

	TC1	TC2	TC3	TC4	TC5
FR1	X		X		
FR2			X		
FR3	X				
FR4			X		
FR5			X		
FR6	X		X		
FR7	X				
FR8		X		X	
FR9				X	
FR10		X			
FR11				X	
FR12		X			
FR13					X
FR14					X

Figure 19-2 An example of a traceability matrix

The level of coverage that must be shown will vary depending on the project. The key is to know what level of coverage must be shown. Traceability can be set up based on the coverage that must be shown. In many cases coverage may be shown by leveraging traces between other artifacts. If a test traces to a specific requirement and that requirement traces to a design element which in turns traces to code, that link may be good enough to show traceability from the test to code that implements the requirement.

Other Things To Trace

Traceability can show that the right things were developed. Systems that support regulations or processes that conform to regulations can use traceability to show requirements were derived from regulations. In such cases traceability is taken beyond requirements and conventional software development artifacts.

An example of this would be a project developing software within the pharmaceutical industry where requirements must support Standard Operation Procedures (SOPs). In this regulated industry, business processes are based on SOPs that must be followed. Systems created to support those business processes must be able to prove they also support the SOPs.

Using traceability to tie the Use Cases (or other forms of requirements) to SOPs is an obvious way of showing correspondence.

In most cases SOPs will be captured on a company intranet or in text documents. It would be cumbersome and a duplication of effort to treat the SOPs as a type of requirement so that they may be traced in a tool. A simpler way of showing this type of traceability would be to treat the SOPs as references to requirements. This is a less formal means of traceability that can be easily done within almost any environment being used for traceability. All the expensive requirements management tools allow for referencing web pages or documents from requirements.

Referencing can also be done with less formal tools that may be used for traceability such as spreadsheets. This is an easy way of showing traceability to other artifacts that must be supported without making them formal requirements. A drawback to this approach is that you won't have the luxury of easily identifying suspect traces that tools provide when artifacts change. This is a tradeoff that needs to be considered when determining not only what will be traced but how to manage the traces.

Traceability In Practice

There are two main benefits to tracing between project artifacts.

A Requirements Perspective

The first is being able to understand project elements the requirements map to such as where the requirements came from (tracing requirements from features and stakeholder needs), and where they lead to in the development process (tracing to design, code, and tests).

- For testing, tracing helps identify what needs to be tested, and demonstrates the test coverage of the requirements.
- By understanding the other artifacts requirements map to, it is easier to understand exactly what needs to be tested to provide the proper testing depth.
- When selecting tests and prioritizing requirements for testing, knowing the other artifacts related to a given requirement may shed light on their importance. A requirement may look trivial on the surface, but may trace to a design element that is critical to system operation or uses an unproven technology. If so, the importance (and priority) of that requirement may be considerably increased.
- Requirements supporting features important to stakeholders may be identified for special testing based on the features they trace from.

- Missing tests can be identified where critical requirements do not trace to any tests.
- Tracing may help identify some tests that don't map to any requirements, and so are, perhaps, unnecessary. That may sound funny, but it happens. Often a tester with a misguided sense of stakeholder perspective gets the idea that a particular test is needed. Once the tests are mapped to requirements, it is found that the test really doesn't test any real requirements.

The Impact of Change

The second benefit comes when analyzing the impact requirement changes have on other artifacts in the development process, not just on testing.

- In general, a good reason to trace is to see where requirements go to and come from. This allows management to understand the effect requirements have on other project artifacts.

Once you document the artifacts a requirement maps to, you can identify the impacts when the requirement changes.

When a requirement changes, its links to other artifacts become suspect. From a testing perspective, if a requirement changes, you need to check each test artifact related to the requirement.

War Story

I worked on a project with a company that subcontracted the testing effort of a large project. We were responsible for identifying, selecting, and creating tests for the system being constructed based on the requirements. We were also responsible for running tests and reporting results.

continued...

Once requirements stabilized and were baselined, we identified and selected tests and then mapped tests to requirements and corresponding design items where pertinent. As tests were created, requirements were clarified and updated based on our suggestions.

After the initial tests were created and run, it became apparent to our client that the product they were producing didn't match all of the stakeholder expectations. This caused a flurry of activity by the client in the form of changing requirements supported by corresponding development.

Suddenly we were deluged with new and changing requirements causing changes to the test suite we had developed so far. This wouldn't have been a big deal had we not contracted the project on a fixed bid. At that point our biggest concern was that the client met their deadline doing whatever we could to help.

Being naïve, we figured we could adjust the contract when the dust settled. So we made changes to our tests and added tests where needed to match the changes in requirements, tested our tests, updated traces and ran the tests to prove the system.

When the dust did settle we found ourselves on the short end of the stick. The client thanked us for the hard work but wasn't willing to pay us for the added costs due to changes. In fact they maintained that those changes were just part of the way they did business and we should have factored that into the contract.

We were maintaining traceability and thought that would help us in our dispute. The problem was that even though we were mapping requirements to Test Cases, we were not keeping track of the history related to mappings and changes. So the only thing we really could tell from our traceability was that the tests traced to the proper artifacts.

Our lesson learned from this episode was that we could have used traceability to manage changes if we were smart.

continued...

We should have put a clause in the contact relating to an expected number of requirements changes after requirements were baselined. As changes came in we could have used existing traces to testing artifacts to help estimate costs related to specific requirement changes.

Problems With Traceability - And Some Suggested Solutions

There are two major pitfalls associated with traceability.

- There is often a tendency to want to trace too much. This is true for organizations tracing artifacts for the first time, and especially true when a new tool is introduced. Usually this can be tempered by carefully considering why traces between specific artifacts should exist and be maintained.
- Another problem is maintaining traceability, especially on large projects with lots of requirements and a large number of artifacts to maintain traces with. As a project progresses and changes occur, it becomes more difficult to manage traceability even with decent tools. Often projects underestimate the amount of work it takes to maintain traceability. When that happens, if more time and effort isn't allotted to managing traceability, the project runs the risk that traces between artifacts will deteriorate and become unreliable, causing more problems than solving. On large projects managing traces may require multiple individuals full time.

Finding the right fit of traceability depends on project needs and requires some planning up front. Ask yourself

- What really needs to be traced?
- Who will be responsible for tracing and when they will do it?

- How traceability will be managed?

What Really Needs To Be Traced?

The stakeholders usually dictate the amount of traceability on a project, whether they know it or not. We employ traceability to help produce a quality product that meets the expectations of the stakeholders. Traceability may also be used to assure stakeholders that the system was tested to the proper level of detail.

On projects with a high degree of governance, traceability needs are usually clearly defined although often extensive. For safety critical development regulated by an organization such as the FAA, requirements must be traced up to system level requirements that describe the entire hardware / software system. They must also trace down to low level (design level) requirements, source code modules, and tests.

For projects with less governance, the project team may have more leeway in establishing traceability. Ask what added value tracing between specific artifacts will bring and if it is necessary.

When deciding on using traceability for test coverage, first understand the degree of test coverage that must be shown to the stakeholders, and whether traceability proof is expected. Next understand the value that employing traceability will provide in ensuring proper test coverage. Then figure out what artifacts must be traced to demonstrate test coverage.

Tracing artifacts can be an expensive overhead, so it is important to try to minimize tracing to only those elements that will produce value in the form of more efficiency or a higher confidence level in the system by the stakeholders.

Before deciding on what will be traced consider tradeoffs between value added and what tracing will cost you in time and complexity. I always try to lean towards less tracing at first and add more if I see it is needed later. This allows me to keep complexity low initially, and adding more tracing (and complexity) only when I can clearly see the value.

Who Will Do The Tracing And When

Once it is known what will be traced, decide who will be doing the tracing.

I choose the people who get the most value from the tracing whenever possible. This will help ensure that tracing takes place when it adds substantial value. People will carefully consider how much value tracing really adds when they are the ones who will have to do the work themselves.

Of course, while that's a nice way to determine who will do the tracing, it isn't always practical.

So in addition, look that those who know the most about the traces and whether managing traceability is the best use of their time. A tester who is building tests against requirements would be the ideal person to handle the traces between test and requirements, since that person is close to both artifacts. In that case the test group may get the most value from that type of trace.

But what if the testing group gets the most value from showing traceability between requirements and design artifacts to the stakeholders to help prove the system? That doesn't mean you want the test people handling that particular trace. The designers would most likely be the best candidates for that task.

When to trace is equally important; the artifacts being traced should be in a fairly stable state. This will help reduce changes in traces once they are enacted. Milestones and baselines are good places to consider tracing. If requirements go through a formal process where they are accepted and baselined, it is wise to wait until those events take place before starting tracing. The same goes for other artifacts as well. Not all projects have the luxury of formal milestones so it may be required to determine when artifacts are stable enough for tracing. The metrics applied to help make the determination will depend on project dynamics. Start thinking about this early as you plan.

Whether/What Tools To Use In Managing Traceability

How traceability will be managed depends on the tracing tools available and their capability, as well as the project and IT environment, such as other tools being used on the project and the standard toolset mandated by a client.

Requirements management tools can be expensive, so think carefully about what a tool will save you as far as time and management complexity. And tools shouldn't make our real jobs more difficult.

War Story

I worked on a project where we were given requirements to test against without a lot of lead time. We did some quick planning and knew what we had to do and also knew what needed to be traced to prove test coverage. We didn't have a tool or method for managing traceability. There was a tool available to us that was being used in other parts of the organization and wouldn't cost us anything. The only problem was that the ramp up effort to get the requirements into the tool, train people on the tool, and ensure it was being used properly was too much for the value we would get.

Meanwhile, the testing manager was a spreadsheet wizard who completely understood our traceability requirements and the skill level of the testing group. He spent half a day putting together a spreadsheet that met our minimum needs and was easy to use by the testing team. This got us going quickly, was good enough, and was the most efficient solution available to us.

First look at what is being used presently. This may be good enough. You may have nothing more than spreadsheets available or nothing at all.

Alternatively, look at what may be readily available to you, for example tools being used in other parts of the organization. But be careful with available licenses and learning curves.

Besides understanding what you have available, taking into account cost and usability, think about the environment a tool will be used in. For example, artifacts are not always in a single repository and may be scattered across various tools and formats. The difficulty of tracing across environments and repositories may cause you to rethink the value of some traces.

Another War Story

I worked with a group that was putting together a requirements management and traceability strategy. The organization had a requirements management tool that most people in the organization were familiar with. This tool was flexible and met most of the organization's needs.

The group decided on a traceability strategy for the organization that included tracing requirements to design items. In anticipation of this strategy the group purchased three seats of a design tool that allowed easy traceability between design objects and requirements in the existing requirements management tool. They figured they had everything they needed to support their strategy.

However, the design and development team were using other tools, including a spreadsheet to show some semblance of tracing from requirements to design that worked well for them, including documenting the design in a text document.

continued...

They had no interest in using a new tool. The design toolset supported a different methodology than was currently being used, and if the requirements management group wanted to convert the design team over to the new tool many more seats of the new design tool would be needed along with lots of training. So a decision was made to hold off on a new design tool and keep the present form of design traceability for the short term. Other alternatives would be evaluated in the future. Although the solution wasn't close to the vision of design element traceability the requirements management group had in mind, it was the best short term alternative to standing an organization on its head and forcing a tool on them that they didn't need.

Conclusion

To Sum Up.

Sure traceability is useful on projects, and even mandatory on some, but make sure you understand what you need it for and how it fits with the organization. Coverage needs must be fully understood and minimized. Traceability can be difficult to enact and manage on large projects so having good reasons for the traceability planned and keeping it to a minimum is essential. Tools can help manage traceability but it is important to understand how tools fit into the environment and whether they help or hinder.

Chapter 20

It All Comes Together Like This

We have covered everything I think is most important about testing. Now I am going to use a case study to try to bring everything covered into perspective. For this example we will use the testing of a system residing on a large jet airplane that must be certified by the FAA. This example should exercise most aspect of agility and Essential Testing. One reason for using a FAA certification example is because testing in regulated environments is becoming more of a reality every day and the FAA is one of the most demanding environments for proving safety.

Situation

A company is building cockpit instrument application that displays instruments on a display panel and allows pilots to perform functions related to the displayed instruments such as fuel load balancing, adjusting cabin temperature and pressure, and control external heaters and deicers.

We have been contracted to do the verification portion of the project which will include verification planning, identifying, selecting, and creating tests against high and low level requirements, provide proof that all requirements are covered by tests, prove that every line of code was tested and that all existing code is accessed. Code inspections must take place to prove coding standards have been followed and the system adequately supports safety standards.

Planning documents have been created for the project with the exception of the verification plan which we will be responsible for.

Requirements are being derived from a system specification supplied by the aircraft manufacturer, limited customer interviews, display standards, and interface documents. The requirements are about 70% complete and are expected to be ready for review prior to test development.

The deadline for development is tight. The development team felt they couldn't wait for the requirements to be complete and began designing and developing the system.

A simulator is currently available to feed inputs into the system under test and review results. At this time quite a bit of manual interaction is involved. We are allowed to modify the tool to allow test automation if it will save testing time.

Our first deliverable will be the verification plan.

First steps

Understanding who will accept the system

The primary stakeholder for this project is the FAA. That is who we must certify the system. The FAA has high standards so testing and proving the system takes a lot of work. The good thing is that this stakeholder is clear on what it takes to prove the system In this case we are certifying the system to a safety level of A. This is the FAA's highest level of safety. To help us understand the FAA's expectations, the client has a Designated Engineering Representative (DER) to work with the project team to ensure we are meeting the FAA's expectations.

The secondary stakeholder is the company responsible for the entire jet being developed. They have system level requirements that must be met by the system we are testing.

They expect the product to meet the system level requirements while integrating with the rest of the jet.

Understand what needs to be done

We have a fair understanding of what needs to be done. It was outlined in the contract. Our group has done this type of verification for others many times before and we have our own processes and templates. Project details are not yet known and we don't know exactly how we are going to make this project a success. We need to understand the customer's processes and how we fit in.

Fortunately the client is in the same city as we are. The project lead for this verification process calls up the overall project manager for the client and offers to spend a week at the client site to help organize certification documents. Since our company has participated is all aspects of certification we can lend our expertise to organize the project. This accomplishes a number of things. First it builds goodwill between us and the client. Helping them with things that are clearly outside the contract shows we are ready to help wherever we can while adding value to the overall project. It also allows us to get into their environment so that we can get a feel for their corporate culture, how they operate, and the other members of the overall project team. This will allow us to open up channels of communication within the organization. Finally, the verification lead will be able to get a clear understanding of details related to what needs to be done and a feel for how we can get the job done efficiently.

It may seem like sending a highly skilled individual to help a client with no extra compensation is a foolish business move, but the communication value we gain is worth it. Since our first effort is to build a detailed verification plan we rely on a few key client contacts to provide us information, and their perspective of the project. By having a person on site we have a chance to get a much broader perspective and better information to plan with.

Understand the environment

The verification manager spends a week at the client's site. While there he does the work he promised. As part of that work he must spend quite a bit of time with the DER reviewing planning documents. This person is very important to projects requiring FAA certification because the individual acts as the eyes of the FAA and knows what the FAA is looking for. Unfortunately, each DER caries their own biases that can weigh heavily on what official artifacts are produced and how they are presented.

From working with the DER our verification manager finds the following:

- The DER is not comfortable with Use Cases and wants to see traditional requirements. If Use Cases are used in the process, they shouldn't be a part of any deliverables.
- Full traceability is expected and will be carefully evaluated.
- High level requirements will be expected to trace up to system requirements.
- High level requirements must trace to low level requirements unless code can be written directly from the information they provide. In those cases they will also be considered low level requirements.
- Low level requirements must trace to modules in the code.
- High level requirements not tracing to low level requirements must trace to code as well.
- All code modules must be trace to by requirements.
- All requirements must trace to tests.

The verification manager also spent time walking around informally talking to individuals on the projects. Here is what he found out:

Requirements

The requirements team is relatively green consisting of a lead with two years experience and two people fresh out of college.

About 70% of an estimated 1500 high level requirements have been written, but haven't been formally reviewed. Looking at a sample of the requirements the verification lead felt the requirements still needed a lot of work before they were testable.

Requirements are being written as traditional requirements and are currently grouped by functionality (instruments being displayed).

There are no plans on the part of the requirements team to use Use Cases to help group requirements. Nobody on the team has experience using them and feels using them would only slow them down.

The requirements lead is under pressure to quickly deliver high level requirements and is worried that the team is going to get hammered when the requirements are presented in formal reviews.

Development

The development team is made up of about eight individuals with varying levels of experience. Many have developed systems similar to this one and are familiar with the underlying architecture.

The team is under the gun to deliver the product on time and couldn't wait for all the requirements to be delivered. So the team has created most of the design and has begun coding based on the system level specification, interface documents, and what high level requirements have been created.

Functionality based on instrument displays has been assigned to individuals. These individuals will participate in requirements reviews related to their assignments. Architectural components have also been assigned to individuals and work has begun.

The development team is worried about the quality of the high level requirements and feels that the requirements team needs to come to them to get clarification on many of the requirements since they are already writing the code.

The team is stressed out and overworked.

The development team has a simulator they built for a previous project that does a decent job of simulating input data from other systems. They plan to make some minor changes so that it may be used on this project. Right now this tool works well for unit testing but may not be ideal for black box testing since it requires a large amount manual interaction.

What we would like changed

There is a lot we would like to change. First off we are scheduled to start work toward creating tests in a week, but would like stable requirements to work with. We are afraid we won't get testable requirements anytime soon. We would like to change the requirements delivery process for rapid delivery of small amounts of requirements as they become available.

We would like to change the requirements process to incorporate Use Cases as a means of grouping requirements.

We would like the simulator tool to be modified to allow for automated testing.

We would like the project team to take a proactive approach to traceability. This could include a clear picture of who will do the tracing and when or possibly assigning someone full time to manage it. Experience tells us that management of so many traces with a large amount of requirements could get out of control if we don't aggressively address it.

We would like the developers to wait until requirements are delivered before they start design and development.

What we can change

We can't change anything to exactly the way we want but there are things we can do to make the testing run smoother.

We would like Use Cases to be part of the project, but know the DER won't go for it. So we will have to create them for our own use as interim artifacts. These will be used to produce artifacts the DER wants to see. We will keep the "Test" Use Cases under the radar.

The requirements team knows they are in trouble but can't see a way out. They are all for providing quick deliveries of small amounts of requirements but don't see the value since that won't improve the quality. They still need to stick to plans of reviewing requirements by functionality group.

We could send our senior requirements person, Sally, over to work with them for two weeks to help get requirements in order. The requirements team is open to this idea. We will have to get involved with requirements sooner or later anyway. Our plan is to let Sally review high level requirements a little at a time from each functional area. Reviewing small amounts will allow for quick feedback to the requirements team and hopefully create a rhythm. While there, we expect Sally to get feedback from the developers. This will help us understand how far off the requirements and the code being developed are, allow for valuable input into the requirements, and foster some teamwork between groups. While doing this Sally can also begin creating Use Cases which is a task we need to do for ourselves. We don't need to share the Use Cases unless it would help move things along. As requirements become clean, Sally can send them to our team that will build the tests for their informal review.

Although we would like the developers to change their process to wait for requirements we know there is no way that is going to happen. What we can do is involve them as much as possible in our requirement activities so that they can be kept up to date on the requirements we will be testing against. This includes helping the requirements team get clean requirements to the developers as they become available. Our test developers will need to communicate with the developers on a regular basis. While much of the communication will be focused on testing, requirements will be addressed as well.

The development team doesn't have time to make any major changes to the simulation tool related to automation, but are willing to let us make changes. We will take a look at the tool to determine the effort and cost/benefit of making the changes.

We talked to the project manager for the client about a clear approach to traceability. At this point the client is reluctant to go into great detail on tracing roles. We do know the client will be using a tool widely used in the industry. While we aren't crazy over the tool, we have a lot of experience with it and know how it can best be used. We send the client some processes and procedures we have used in the past for using the tool for the type of traceability planned. We are still concerned about traceability.

At this point it looks like we are going to be spending a lot of time on work unrelated to our specific duties of verifying a system. We don't see a problem with that. We calculate the work we are taking on early in the project will reduce project risks and improve the quality of artifacts that we require to do our job. This should help improve our efficiency over the course of the project.

The decisions made so far relating to identifying potential problems and taking action within our power to proactively address them are based on experience. This is important to note because taking these types of actions require confidence that is usually gained by experience. We also know that as we make these decisions, we are also making mistakes. That is ok by us, because once we realize our mistakes we will fix them. One of the concepts of Essential Testing is that you do what it takes to do your job as efficiently as possible. Accepting the current situation isn't an option if you know it is sub optimal.

Test Planning

During the first week, we send Sally, the requirements expert, to the client's site, while we prepare the verification plan. A template for the plan is available and it outlines major testing milestones, deliverables, and testing activities. This is adjusted to the present project.

Identifying the Artifacts we will use

As one of the first steps of test planning we identify inputs we plan to use in the testing process. Based on development documentation we know what formal artifacts the project will create that will be available for us to use. The major artifacts that we will use include High Level requirements, low level requirements, the source code, software builds, and artifact traces. We will also be using coding standards, deign standards, and the system level specification.

High level requirements will be used to write tests against. These requirements will be presented formally in a System Requirements Document, but our main access to the requirements will be in the requirements management tool. The system level specification created by the jet builder will be used to help understand the context of the high level requirements and to help identify safety related tests. These will be part of a formal Software Design Document (SDD) and will also be accessible via the requirements management tool. The SDD will be used to understand the context of the low level requirements we will be writing tests against.

Code inspections will be performed against the code to verify safety. The source code will also be used for understanding as we build tests. Software builds will be used to run tests against in order to verify the system. We will also instrument the code with a coverage tool to verify complete coverage.

Identifying the artifacts we will create

Also early in the test planning process we identify the outputs we will create. Besides the artifacts we will present as proof the product was tested properly and works, we will also identify interim artifacts used to create the final product. These will help us map out process details later. The goal is to keep the artifact list as small as possible. We want to identify only things that will directly contribute to the proof of the system. Unfortunately, the list tends to be rather large for safety critical projects like this.

The primary artifacts that will be presented to the customer and the FAA include black box tests against high level requirements and many low level requirements, White box tests against the remaining low level requirements, proof of test coverage of requirements via traceability, test results, defect reports, proof code follows safety standards, and proof of code coverage by tests. Tests will consist of written Test Procedures, test input files, and any associate automated tests.

Interim artifacts will include Use Case Specifications to help us group requirements, Operational Variable tables, variant tables for identifying tests. We also anticipate creating a spreadsheet that will include our assumptions related to the requirements.

Lay out the test process

Now that we understand our environment, know what inputs we will be using and what we must produce to prove the system,, we can lay out a process that will get us there. As we do this we need to keep in mind that we are just creating a guide to get us started. We can't anticipate everything and we most certainly will make mistakes. So if we are unsure of some details, we will take our best guess and worry about it later.

Start with what we know

We start with what we know the stakeholders want. Our organization has done quite a bit verification of systems certified by the FAA, so it is understood what is important to the FAA. We have already incorporated details related to artifacts to be produced in our verification plan template.

We also want to use things that have worked for us in the past. In our case, we are very comfortable with Use Case driven testing. We will adapt our existing Use Case based testing processes to the current situation. Since Use Cases are not considered requirements for the project, we will have to include activities to create Use Cases to group requirements, and map tests to traditional tests. We have tools and methodologies in place for coverage analysis, code inspection, and test execution and reporting. We will have to tweak these somewhat to match the situation.

Consider patterns

Under other circumstances we would use test patterns that help us reduce the number of tests to run. In this case however, those patterns won't do us any good since the FAA expects complete requirements/code test coverage for level A certification.

We have considered the Extended Use Case Test Design pattern for identifying tests and plan to modify it to fit our needs. This process will be detailed in the Test Plan. This is also called a "Verification" plan by the FAA.

Start with the input documents and map out the process

At this point we have a pretty clear idea of what processes and methodology we are going to use to get the job done. Now we have to lay out the details. We start with the inputs and work our way through the process doing only what is necessary to produce the outputs we need to prove the system.

We start with the requirement as inputs. First we will look at high level requirements. These are the requirements we will perform black box testing against. Here are the steps we will use to identify tests from the requirements.

Create Use Cases

We know we are going to base our tests on Use Cases, so we will need to create Use Cases to group requirements. We can start with the major features the high level requirements are categorized by (instrument displays) and identify initial Use Cases. We will also use the system specification and insight from the requirements analysts and developers to get an understanding of the Actors and their interaction with the system. Use Case details will be created and the Use Cases will be peer reviewed by other test personnel.

Group and Verify Requirements

Requirements will be grouped by Use Cases. Since Use Cases are not official documents for this project we won't use the requirements management tool to trace. We will manage the relationship with a spreadsheet. The test designers will each be assigned Use Cases to create tests. Each test designer will be responsible for mapping high level requirements to their Test Cases. As requirements are grouped, the test designers will also inspect requirements for testability. Although we anticipate a great deal of informal interaction between test and the requirements analysts to address changes to requirements, the plan will only address the formal process.

Identify tests

We plan to use a process based on the Extended Use Case Test design pattern to identify and select tests. The plan is written to describe the process in detail. We plan to identify Operational Variables from the Use Cases and associate conditions that could cause significant behavior from the system. We will then build variant tables that combine combinations of specific conditions of Operational Variables. These will be our potential tests. We will then review high level requirements related to the Use Cases and select tests from the variant table to cover the requirements. We will then add tests to fill in gaps.

Identify additional tests

Not all requirements will map to Use Cases. There will also be non-functional requirements to deal with. For these we will have to identify Test Cases. We will reference detailed activities to perform for this task in the verification plan.

Create black box Tests

For this project there are no existing tests that can be used. We will have to create all tests from scratch. We will have to make some assumptions about the simulation tool in order to identify the steps for creating black box tests. We want to automate the tests as much as possible. We are going to try to make adjustments to the tool to interact with automated scripts, but we don't know that we will be successful. So for now we will define a process for creating manual tests. If it turns out that we can easily automate later on, we will change the process. We create Test Procedure and Test Case templates to be used to create manual tests and reference them in the verification plan.

Identify white box tests

Now we focus on the low level requirements. As we implement the Test Plan there are still unknowns related to the low level requirements. We are not completely clear what they look like or the quality we can expect. We will describe activities for the formal acceptance of the low level requirements, but have to add activities for further review to ensure testability. We expect the low level requirements will be officially accepted and baselined before they are really ready in order to meet deadlines. We won't put that in the Test Plan but we will add some steps that will help us deal with the situation.

Design tests

We would like to take advantage of processes our team is familiar with and will use processes we already have. Test design will consist of reviewing the Use Cases and the selected tests to group tests by Use Case flow. Each of these groupings will make up a Test Case. Additional Test Cases will be identified to cover any remaining selected tests. Test Cases will be filled out for each identified Test Case using a Test Case template. As part of the Test Case, Activity Diagrams will be used to show how the test will be flow.

Create tests

Test Procedures will be created for each Test Case using a template. Since we have the initial test environment available to us, it will be possible to dry run tests to make sure they make sense. We will schedule peer reviews in the form of inspecting and running through the flow of the tests. We feel the most efficient way to review tests is to have team members swap tests with other team members for inspections. This will allow a single reviewer for each Test Case rather than having groups of individuals reviewing the same tests. If the team was less experienced, group reviews would make sense at first in order to get a level of consistency.

Trace tests

We don't yet have all the details related to traceability so we will make some assumption. We don't want to do anymore than we have to - so we concern ourselves only with tracing test coverage to requirements - for now. We put in the plan that once tests have been created team members will be responsible for importing Test Procedures into the requirements management tool and trace them to requirements.

Executing tests

The project is taking an approach where the development team will deliver builds to us and we will test increasing amounts of functionality on each build. Once the final build is released we will test remaining functionality, make sure bugs are fixed, make final adjustments to tests and send all tests to the client so that they can perform final test. The verification plan will have defect severity information and acceptance criteria.

Coverage analysis

We know that the FAA expects Modified Condition/Decision Coverage for Level A software. We know which tool we will be using for coverage analysis, and how we plan to use it and report results. We describe all these details in the verification plan.

Code Verification

Code verification will be required for some robustness testing and ensuring that the code meets safety standards. We will need source code as well as coding standards and safety standards for this task.

Based on all the above information we are able to create a verification plan with all pertinent details relating tools, test types, and standards. The review is scheduled for the following week.

Requirements help and Use Cases creation

While the test group is putting together the Test Plan, Sally, our requirements expert is working on site with the client and is having mixed results.

Sally begins by reviewing small amounts of requirements from each functional category. This allows for quick feedback to the requirements analysts so that requirements they produce in the future meet our expectations. This works and the new requirements begin to improve.

Toward the end of the first week Sally had identified initial Use Cases for the system and had brief descriptions for each. She found that the Use Cases painted a better picture of the system than the functional categories and didn't always line up with the categories. She approached the requirements analysts to see if it was possible to regroup requirements. While they liked the way the Use Cases grouped the requirements, the answer was no. This would have made it easier for us to map requirements when identifying tests, but won't pose any real problems or significantly slow us down.

Early in the second week Sally participates in the first preliminary review of a group of requirements related to the cabin pressure display. The developer responsible for delivering cabin pressure functionality also participated. Many problems were found and the requirements analyst resolved to fix most of them before the official review. While Sally was more concerned with understandability, many of the problems the developer cited were related to stated functionality not matching what he was developing. The requirements analyst didn't challenge the developer on any of the comments.

In the middle of the second week the requirements analysts announced that their original process for requirements approval was changing slightly. Instead of a traditional review where there is a scribe and moderator, and everyone meets in person to discuss problems found with the requirements, the reviewers would email comments to the requirements analyst and that person would respond by either challenging the comments or make the changes. The time between publishing the requirements and when comments were due was also reduced from 3 days to 1. This was proposed to reduce the time to approve a group of requirements. We are skeptical and protest to the project manager. We get shot down. By the end of the week the first group of requirements has been "approved" and baselined.

Sally's two weeks are up and she returns from the client site. She announces that she can't take it anymore. She will leave the company after this project to pursue her dream of becoming a figure skating columnist.

It is now clear to us that the requirements will not be of the quality we wanted. We talk to the requirements lead and the project manager and work an agreement where our testers will review the approved requirements as they develop tests, and make suggestions for clarity. These suggestions will be discussed with the requirements analysts, changes can be made, and a second baseline of requirements will take place later in the project. The requirements analysts are agreeable to this because now they can get deliverables out initially so that testers and developers can use them, and they get some help in writing clear requirements. The project manager is agreeable because he knows the requirements being baselined now are not going to be good enough to drive the rest of the project and to present to the jet builder for final review. The requirements will be formally presented to the jet builder once the second baseline takes place. That means there is only about a month before the second baseline. This isn't much time, but we should be able to make significant progress with both requirements and tests during that time… And the entire team has started to demonstrate an ability to be Agile.

Identify tests by Use Case

Use Cases are created with quite a bit of interaction with the requirements analysts and developers. We find that we are asking questions related to the context in which the functionality is performed, but that hasn't been considered yet. This causes the requirements analysts to rethink some of the requirements and spurs more questions for the jet maker to answer. Most of our questions are answered. For the questions not resolved, we make assumptions and note them in the Use

Case Specification. The Use Cases are then peer reviewed. We now have Use Cases good enough to drive testing.

We get the first groups of initially baselined high level requirements to identify and build tests against. It looks like we have a significant amount of work required to clarify the requirement so we change our process slightly to accommodate less than ideal high level requirements. We were planning on using a spreadsheet to map the requirements to Use Cases. We add some steps to first put the requirements into the spreadsheet and add another column for suggested requirements. The test designers then review each requirement. If the requirement needs to be clarified, the test designer modifies or rewrites the requirement and places the results into the suggestion column. Use Cases are identified for each requirement. In some cases requirements map to multiple Use Cases/steps. Test designers send the spreadsheet with the suggested changes to the requirements analysts on a daily basis. Discussions on the changes take place as needed. With the first set of requirements we found that the requirements analysts were more than happy to take our suggestions at face value and make the changes.

As requirements are mapped we begin the process to identify tests which includes identifying Operational Variables in a table and then creating variant tables.

We don't wait for the high level requirements to get started with the test identification process. Test designers that have not yet received delivered requirements for the functionality related to their assigned Use Cases start creating Operational Variables. We don't need the requirements to get started since we have confidence in the Use Cases. We use the Use Cases, unofficial requirements passed on to us by the requirements team, and discussions with developers and requirements analysts to identify potentially important conditions for each Operational Variable. We can create the initial format of the variant tables for the Use Case, but hold off on filling in much of the details until the official requirements are delivered. Each test designer has enough Use Cases to keep busy creating Operational Variable tables until the official requirements are delivered.

So we get heavily involved in test identification process and most of the requirements are initially baselined and delivered. We continue to make requirement change suggestions as we go. If we had already started identifying Operational Variables we review and update them based on the delivered requirements. Variant tables are built for each Use Case and each variant is numbered. We review the requirements against the discovered variants and select the variants we need to cover requirements. We add another column to our spreadsheet to show variants corresponding to the requirements as they are selected. This will allow us to map requirements to tests later on.

Low Level Requirements delivered

The development team asks us to review the Software Design Document (SDD) to confirm their interpretation of Low Level requirements. This is very informal, but it helps get us on the same page. It turns out the low level requirements are in pretty good shape, but it is unclear how easily they will trace to the high level requirements. The development team will begin moving identified Low Level requirements into the requirements management tool and formally delivering them to us. We offer to help them trace the High Level Requirements to Low Level, although the development team will be responsible for maintaining traceability in the tool. We have to understand the links anyway in order to create additional tests for test coverage.

As low level requirements are delivered we review them against the high level requirements in our spreadsheet and any corresponding tests we are creating. We add yet another column to our spreadsheet for low level requirements identifier. In that column we identify the low level requirements that correspond to high level requirements. We can present this information to the developers to aid in their traceability effort.

Any low levels that do not trace to high level requirements are examined and tests are identified to address them. These are identified in a list for now with corresponding Low Level requirements.

As we design the tests for High Level requirements we will take a closer look at any related low level requirements to see if our tests can cover those as well. We will identify any additional tests at that point. Chances are those will be white box tests.

We keep adding onto this informal spreadsheet as needed. This is the easiest way for us to keep track of things by requirements as we identify tests. As we use it, we can hide columns we don't need at the time. It is also useful for presenting information to the requirements analysts and developers. This is just an interim artifact and we are not worried about keeping all traces up to date in the long run. That will happen in the requirements management tool.

Requirements Baselined for 2nd time

As we move deeper into test identification the High Level requirements are baselined for the second time. The deadline came to meet with the jet builder and the requirements were reviewed and accepted. The quality of the requirements is much better now, but we still have some outstanding questions that haven't been addressed and a small number of requirements we haven't reviewed yet. We are told that the requirements team will not be clarifying our requirements any longer. We have been maintaining our spreadsheet by periodically importing the high level requirements from the requirements management tool. We instruct the test designers to review the spreadsheet and clean up the column for suggested requirements changes to only include any unaddressed suggestions.

Some of the test designers are not sure what to do with unclear requirements not addressed. They have gotten used to getting the changes they requested. The test lead instructs the team to write any discrepancies in the suggestion field of the spreadsheet and move on. We will continue to present the spreadsheet to the requirements analysts, the development team and the project manager for feedback and to express our interpretation of the requirements. Only for now on, we only expect confirmation or clarification of the requirements with no official action. We want to make sure everyone knows how we are interpreting requirements to build our tests. We will update the suggestion field for the common understanding of the unclear requirement and use that to build our tests. When we present our tests we will also present our interpretation of the requirements.

Design tests

Tests are selected from the variant tables and grouped into what we call Test Cases that combine tests that can be run together. Each test designer is responsible for identifying the Test Cases for their assigned Use Cases.

The process to design a Test Case consists of reviewing the tests that will be included from the variant tables along with corresponding requirements and filling out a Test Case template. The high and low level requirements the Test Case addresses are identified in the document. This helps us in the design process. As the Test Case is built, the test designer determines if the requirements are sufficiently tests. Any additional tests are identified. The white box tests identified for low level requirements will be address later.

The test designers create Activity Diagrams to outline the test process and responsibilities. At this point the progress in modifying the simulation tool to enhance automation is moving slowly. So the test designers will design the tests around the current version of the tool which means more manual interaction.

The design moves forward rapidly. The tests cases are peer reviewed as they are created. Once Test Procedures are peer reviewed they are ready to be used in test creation.

Develop tests

Using the Test Procedure template the test designers create the tests based on the Test Cases. They use a template for a Test Procedure includes test set up instructions, step-by-step procedures for running the tests with expected results and pass fail criteria, and test analysis instructions. The Activity Diagrams in the Test Cases are used to help create the tests. The Use Cases are also used to help understand scenarios that will sequential run the tests.

As the procedures are being written we begin to realize how labor intensive it will be to run the tests. As the right resources free up, they are assigned to figure out a way to automate tests. In the mean time the effort to create the tests continues as planned.

Execute Tests

The order of creation of the black box tests were planned to coincide with the delivery of corresponding functionality. The first delivery of functionality takes place and tests are run. We work closely with the developers to work through what we perceive as defects that impede our ability to test. The developers are quick to respond to get the product to a testable state and we are in constant communication with the developers. We notice that many of the defects are due to the developers having a different understanding of the requirements than we did. It turns out that much of the misunderstanding is due to the developers beginning coding before the requirements were ready and not keeping up with requirement changes. The developers eventually resolve the major defects. Once the first build is relatively clean we send our tests to the client so that they can run them to get a feel for what the testing will entail. They run the first batch of tests and their first comment is that the tests take too long to run.

They will only have a couple of days to run the final tests with three testers. They figure the timeframe will be too tight.

At about the same time our team assigned to modifying the simulation tool is making progress and is testing an updated version that allows the acceptance of simple scripts that feed information into the simulator. By this time most of the tests have been created. We make the decision to refactor the existing tests for automation and create the remaining ones for automation. We anticipated that this may happen and feel that the extra work won't be so bad.

Coverage analysis

As we run the tests we find the client isn't able to provide us with the coverage tool yet. They are having trouble instrumenting the code with the tool they purchased. We are not scheduled to perform coverage analysis until the final build but don't want to take any chances. We begin researching alternatives to the chosen tool.

Code Inspections

As we get the first build we begin preliminary code inspections. The bulk of the work is not scheduled until the final build. We are doing the initial code inspections to train personnel on what to look for and to get a feel of the condition of the code. We find that most of the code is in pretty good shape. We inform the development team of the problems we are finding so that they can take action as they continue development.

Create white box tests

As the team completes the black box tests they begin on the white box tests. In many cases this consists of writing code to test specific portions of the design or specific low level requirements.

Refactoring Tests

We finally have the modified version of the simulation tool stable and verified. The team begins changing existing tests.

We find that since we did a good job of writing the original Test Procedures with all the input details, the automation process is fairly strait forward. We have to build scripts and test files for the tests, update the Test Procedures to reflect the automation, and test the new tests by running the old and the new tests to ensure no variations in results. After automating a couple of tests we find that the test execution time is cut significantly while the time to evaluate results is about the same. This makes it well worth the effort.

We continue automating the existing tests as well as the black box tests yet to be completed.

Final build delivered

As builds were being delivered we made adjustments to accommodate expected and unexpected problems that materialized along the way. As delivery of functionality progressed, the quality of the delivered product improved and things seemed to go smoother. The one thing we did notice was that some functionality slated for earlier deliveries was postponed until the final delivery. This concerned us, but there wasn't much we could do. We were able to get the final build date adjusted so that we would have four weeks before code and tests are sent to the client for final test instead of three weeks. This gave us an extra week to test, debug, perform code inspections, and perform coverage analysis.

There was a final push by the development team to get the final functionality delivered on time. The final functionality was delivered on time but at a cost. All process went out the window for the final push. It takes a day to get the product to run on our test environment. It takes another week of working around the clock with the development team to get the regression tests to pass. From there we continue testing new functionality, reporting defects, and retesting bug fixes. The week prior to final testing, the product begins to stabilize with major bugs resolved. We keep a team together to conduct remaining tests and move other team members to help complete coverage analysis and code inspections.

Final coverage analysis

As final functionality is delivered, the client still hasn't got the coverage analysis tool running with delivered code yet. This is a major problem because that is the tool we must use. Fortunately, we started searching for alternative weeks ago and came up with a decent approach. The tool we found was easy to instrument to the code and had decent reporting capabilities. The only problem was that it wasn't qualified with the FAA. That is, the tool hadn't been proven to work properly to the FAA. The tool the client would be supplying had been qualified. The process to qualify the tool would take more time than we have.

We have to get started analyzing coverage. We decided to use the unqualified tool to get started and would use the client supplied tool for final analysis. We got a free 30 day trial version of the coverage tool we would use to do our initial analysis and assigned two individuals to get it running and perform analysis. They were able to begin work on this once the final product was executable.

Initial analysis found that 90% of the code was satisfactorily covered by black box tests. Running the additional white box tests brought that number to 95%. The uncovered code was inspected and the developers confirmed that some of the code was not being used and eliminated it. The test team created white box tests to cover the rest of the uncovered code.

In the last week of delivery the client finally gets the tool working and is ready to run final coverage analysis. We give them all the tests to run, they execute them and the final analysis goes very smoothly since we had already addressed most problems with the use of the unqualified tool.

Traceability

We continued to update our traces in the requirements management tool as changes and additions were made to black box and white box tests. We haven't paid attention to the traceability of the rest of the artifacts. As the final week of testing approaches, project management acknowledges that traceability is a mess. The project manager assigns two requirements analysts too work full time with a developer to redo all traces. The developer is assigned to the effort part time. Since we have quite a bit of experience with traceability, we supply a part time resource to manage an effort. All traces have to be revisited, but the effort pays off, traceability is established, and reports are generated on time.

Follow Up

All deliverables were created and presented on time. There were some flaws discovered by the Jet builder, the client, and the DER. We spend another month resolving issues with the rest of the project team. At this point we have two individuals to manage this effort. The rest of the team has gone on to other things.

Synopsis

Overall the project was a success because it more or less completed on time. Of course, since this is made up, we can create a successful ending. In creating this scenario, I added as much dysfunction and bad things happening as possible with potential solutions. I also tried to base the solutions on environmental conditions related to the project. Real solutions must take into consideration the project environment, experience of the test team and others on the project, and our ability to initiate change. In real life we don't know if the solutions proposed would pan out. The point is to make the choice you think is best to get the job done, and adjust if things don't turn out like you planned.

It can be argued that the test team did a lot of extra work not associated with testing in this scenario. That is certainly true. Many of the activities, such as loaning requirements expertise, helped other groups. In the case of the loan of the requirements analyst there were mixed results. The extra work was done in an effort to make the project a success and to take proactive steps to avoid problems that would directly affect test when we could least afford it.

This example tries to show what Essential Testing is all about. That is to do what it takes to test the right thing to the right level of detail at the right time as efficiently as possible.

Chapter 21

Conclusion

Not long ago I found myself working on a project as a test mentor. (No matter how much I insist I am not a tester I seem to get those engagements!)

I was called into a meeting to discuss changing the direction of testing on a project.

The developers were beginning to deliver code but were late. Since a large part of testing would be delayed and it didn't look like the project allotted enough time for the testing under the current approach, the existing Test Plan would put us months past the implementation date, causing the project to incur penalties.

The project manager wanted to know how we could make changes in the testing approach to cut the time to get to implementation without sacrificing the quality. I sketched out a plan to streamline the way tests would be developed and suggested using a pattern that would allow us to drop low priority tests.

The senior tester was adamant that the Test Plan must stay as is and the end date would just have to be moved back. He continued to lament that the end date was irrational in the first place and that it should come as no surprise that the date would be missed. The same approach to testing was used on the last project, which was late, and the amount of time to develop tests is known.

I wondered to myself why someone would think an approach that didn't work on the last project with similar conditions would work this time.

No decision was made in the meeting. After the meeting I asked the senior tester to come by my cube. I told him I admired the fact that he was willing to stand up for his principles related to software quality and handed him the pair of pliers I received from my friend years ago on my first project as a tester. I told him the story behind them and that I figured he could use them more than I could.

I was going to start the concluding chapter with a story about a group of tester that were proactive in everything they did, saved projects, and were highly regarded by everyone.

Then I figure, why lie?

Much of the premise of this book relates to being proactive and taking our destiny in our own hands as much as possible. That means that, when we test, we will step on toes. Although we can try to minimize the number of toes we step on, there will always be some animosity generated and our efforts will never be fully appreciated.

Accepting that takes courage.

Appendix A

Additional Information for Top Notch Conveyor System

Technical explanation of a typical conveyor system

The following scenario illustrates the path packages that travel a typical Top Notch conveyor system take. Figure A-1 shows the conveyor system.

Pick Station

A typical package is filled with items and sealed at a picking station. At that point, a bar code is produced that indicates the package's destination and a unique identifier. At creation of the barcode, the information is sent to a dispatching application that is responsible for determining the final lane/truck the package will be sent to. The dispatching program is a legacy application that the current conveyor systems interact with. This application will not be rewritten anytime soon although there is a project underway to enhance the application to support web services.

Accumulation

Once a package has been sealed and a barcode has been placed on it, it is placed on a conveyor belt and transported to a location where packages are accumulated. The accumulation process consists of grouping packages into lots and holding the lots until they are to be released into the conveyor system. A typical lot contains ten to twelve packages that are bunched back-to-back in a release area. The lot information is sent to the dispatch application. The final portion of the accumulation process consists of releasing package lots to the main conveyor system. The accumulation process is controlled by an existing system made up of conveyor hardware and a software application. The current accumulation subsystem runs independently of the main conveyor system. There are no immediate plans to change this subsystem functionality. The only changes that would be considered at this time would be communication related to support the new conveyor system.

Induction Merging and Spacing

Once a package is released into the system as part of a lot, it will find its way to one of several induction lanes. (The current system can be configured with one or two lanes only. The new system may have up to five.) The induction process is fairly complex. First a package is recognized by the conveyor system as it passes a package detector. (Current package detectors are photo eyes.) It is also measured. At this point the package is first recognized by the system. The induction line consists of multiple belts. The speed of each belt can be controlled to create space between packages. Each induction lane is responsible for creating spaces between packages. All induction lanes merge into a single lane. A package should arrive at the end of its induction lane in a position to be able to merge into the single lane without running into packages merging from other lanes. This is complex because not only does a package have to be spaced properly with the package in front of it, but must be spaced properly with packages on other lanes. There is an existing spacing algorithm that will have to be incorporated into the new system. While the company has legacy four belt spacing systems (induction lanes), it has just purchased a company that has build the hardware for an eight belt system with different hard sensors. It is felt that if the software is developed correctly, the software controlling the spacing should work with both systems. There will be minor modifications to the lower level sensor software.

Transportation

Once on the single conveyor lane the package should take an uneventful ride toward its final destination. The main concern in this part of the ride is to ensure that nothing bad happens to the package such as jams or changes in its spacing with packages in front and back of it. During this portion of the trip, the package is scanned and the conveyor system accesses the dispatch system to determine the diversion lane destination. The dispatch application determines the lane based on trucks available, and how many packages in the divert lanes. Once a diversion lane has been determined the system will predict when the package will arrive ate the appropriate diversion lane.

Diversion

As a package passes the lane it is to be diverted onto, it is mechanically pushed onto the diversion lane and transported to the final destination where it is loaded onto a truck. After successful diversion, the dispatch system is informed of the success. The current system handles the diversion of packages. There is now new diversion hardware created as a subsystem that is supposed to be better than the existing hardware. The software to support this hardware will be created in a separate project and will not be part of the new conveyor system project. It is understood that the supporting software must communicate with the new conveyor system software.

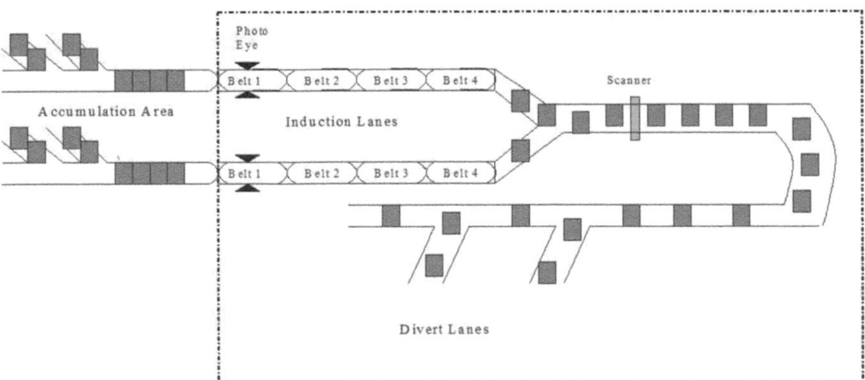

Figure A-1 Example of typical conveyor system

Appendix B Examples

Variant Table example for Open a Lane Basic Flow

The following table represents the entire Variant Table for the example used in chapter 14.

Var.	Sys State	Open Lane Request	Dest. ID	Lane Selection	Package Limit	Open Gate	Gate Response	Expected Results	Comments
1	Operational – lanes available	Valid Request	N/A	N/A	N/A	N/A	N/A	The system prompts for a destination	
2	Operational – lanes available	Invalid Request	N/A	N/A	N/A	N/A	N/A	Not specified	No requirement yet. Consider an off nominal test for now
3	Operational – lanes available	Valid Request	Valid	N/A	N/A	N/A	N/A	The system displays lanes currently assigned to the requested destination and the lanes currently available	
4	Operational – lanes available	Valid Request	Invalid Format	N/A	N/A	N/A	N/A	Error Message returned for invalid format	No requirement
5	Operational – lanes available	Valid Request	Non existent destination	N/A	N/A	N/A	N/A	System responds that couldn't find destination	No requirement
6	Operational – lanes available	Valid Request	Valid	Available lane Selected	Valid	N/A	N/A	The system assigns the lane and prompts to open the gate on the conveyor associated with the lane.	

Var.	Sys State	Open Lane Request	Dest. ID	Lane Selection	Package Limit	Open Gate	Gate Response	Expected Results	Comments
7	Operational – lanes available	Valid Request	Valid	Held Lane selected	Valid	N/A	N/A	The system doesn't allow selection of a held lane	
8	Operational – lanes available	Valid Request	Valid	Assigned lane selected	Valid	N/A	N/A	The system doesn't allow selection of an assigned lane	
9	Operational – lanes available	Valid Request	Valid	Invalid Lane	Valid	N/A	N/A	The system prompts for a valid lane	
10	Operational – lanes available	Valid Request	Valid	No Lane Selected	Valid	N/A	N/A	The system prompts for entry of a lane	
11	Operational – lanes available	Valid Request	Valid	Available lane Selected	Value of 0	N/A	N/A	The system prompts for a value other than 0.	No requirement yet.
12	Operational – lanes available	Valid Request	Valid	Held Lane selected	Value of 0	N/A	N/A	The system doesn't allow selection of a held lane	Two negative values
13	Operational – lanes available	Valid Request	Valid	Assigned lane selected	Value of 0	N/A	N/A	The system doesn't allow selection of an assigned lane	Two negative values
14	Operational – lanes available	Valid Request	Valid	Invalid Lane	Value of 0	N/A	N/A	The system prompts for a valid lane	Two negative values
15	Operational – lanes available	Valid Request	Valid	No Lane Selected	Value of 0	N/A	N/A	The system prompts for entry of a lane	Two negative values
16	Operational – lanes available	Valid Request	Valid	Available lane Selected	Invalid format	N/A	N/A	The system prompts for a valid format	Need a requirement
17	Operational – lanes available	Valid Request	Valid	Available lane Selected	No value entered	N/A	N/A	The system prompts for a value	Need a requirement
18	Operational – lanes available	Valid Request	Valid	Available lane Selected	Valid	Valid	N/A	The system responds by sending a request to the divert lane control system to open the gate.	
19	Operational – lanes available	Valid Request	Valid	Available lane Selected	Valid	Invalid format	N/A	System prompts for valid format	

Var.	Sys State	Open Lane Request	Dest. ID	Lane Selection	Package Limit	Open Gate	Gate Response	Expected Results	Comments
20	Operational – lanes available	Valid Request	Valid	Available lane Selected	Valid	Wrong gate specified	N/A	System indicated the gate cannot be opened and prompts for a different gate.	
21	Operational – lanes available	Valid Request	Valid	Available lane Selected	Valid	No Command	N/A	The system waits for an open command	
22	Operational – lanes available	Valid Request	Valid	Available lane Selected	Valid	Valid	Gate Open	The system: Stores the gate and destination information Sends the Dispatch System with the lane and destination assignment information indicating packages can be assigned to the lane. Notifies the Conveyor Operator	
23	Operational – lanes available	Valid Request	Valid	Available lane Selected	Valid	Valid	Gate Locked Error	The system informs the operator the gate could not be opened	
24	Operational – lanes available	Valid Request	Valid	Available lane Selected	Valid	Valid	No response	After ten seconds the system determines the gate can't be opened and informs the operator	
25	Operational – all lanes held or assigned	Valid Request	N/A	N/A	N/A	N/A	N/A	The system informs the operator that there are no lanes available for assignment	
26	Operational – Destination selected at max assignments	Valid Request	Valid	N/A	N/A	N/A	N/A	The system informs the operator that no lanes can be assigned to that destination.	

Var.	Sys State	Open Lane Request	Dest. ID	Lane Selection	Package Limit	Open Gate	Gate Response	Expected Results	Comments
27	Operational – Selected gate already opened	Valid Request	Valid	Available lane Selected	Valid	Valid	N/A	The system informs the Conveyor Operator that the selected gate is already open	
28	No Communication with Dispatch system	Valid Request	Valid	Available lane Selected	Valid	Valid	Gate Open	Not sure what the response is	No requirement

Table B1 Open a Lane Basic Flow Variant Table

Example of Multiple Variant Tables for a Single Use Case Flow

This is an example of using multiple tables to identify potential tests. The same example for the *Open a Lane* flow as used in chapter 17 is illustrated.

The reason to use multiple tables is for readability.

As mentioned in chapter 17, a good place to split the table is between *Package Limit* and *Open Gate*. This is because *Package Limit* is the last input for the steps leading up to assigning a gate, and *Open Gate* is the first input into the steps related to coordinating the physical opening of a gate. The first table is created the same as in the example for one table in chapter 17 with the exception that there are less operational variables listed. The System State used is the same as in the other example.

Here is the first table

Variant	Sys State	Open Lane Request	Destination ID	Lane Selection	Package Limit	Expected Results	Comments
1	Operational – lanes available	Valid Request	N/A	N/A	N/A	The system prompts for a destination	
2	Operational – lanes available	Invalid Request	N/A	N/A	N/A	Not specified	No requirement yet. Consider an off nominal test for now
3	Operational – lanes available	Valid Request	Valid	N/A	N/A	The system displays lanes currently assigned to the requested destination and the lanes currently available	
4	Operational – lanes available	Valid Request	Invalid Format	N/A	N/A	Error Message returned for invalid format	No requirement
5	Operational – lanes available	Valid Request	Non existent destination	N/A	N/A	System responds that couldn't find destination	No requirement
6	Operational – lanes available	Valid Request	Valid	Available lane Selected	Valid	The system assigns the lane and prompts to open the gate on the conveyor associated with the lane.	
7	Operational – lanes available	Valid Request	Valid	Held Lane selected	Valid	The system doesn't allow selection of a held lane	
8	Operational – lanes available	Valid Request	Valid	Assigned lane selected	Valid	The system doesn't allow selection of an assigned lane	
9	Operational – lanes available	Valid Request	Valid	Invalid Lane	Valid	The system prompts for a valid lane	
10	Operational – lanes available	Valid Request	Valid	No Lane Selected	Valid	The system prompts for entry of a lane	

Variant	Sys State	Open Lane Request	Destination ID	Lane Selection	Package Limit	Expected Results	Comments
11	Operational – lanes available	Valid Request	Valid	Available lane Selected	Value of 0	The system prompts for a value other than 0.	No requirement yet.
12	Operational – lanes available	Valid Request	Valid	Held Lane selected	Value of 0	The system doesn't allow selection of a held lane	Two negative values
13	Operational – lanes available	Valid Request	Valid	Assigned lane selected	Value of 0	The system doesn't allow selection of an assigned lane	Two negative values
14	Operational – lanes available	Valid Request	Valid	Invalid Lane	Value of 0	The system prompts for a valid lane	Two negative values
15	Operational – lanes available	Valid Request	Valid	No Lane Selected	Value of 0	The system prompts for entry of a lane	Two negative values
16	Operational – lanes available	Valid Request	Valid	Available lane Selected	Invalid format	The system prompts for a valid format	Need a requirement
17	Operational – lanes available	Valid Request	Valid	Available lane Selected	No value entered	The system prompts for a value	Need a requirement
18	Operational – all lanes held or assigned	Valid Request	N/A	N/A	N/A	The system informs the operator that there are no lanes available for assignment	
19	Operational – Destination selected at max assignments	Valid Request	Valid	N/A	N/A	The system informs the operator that no lanes can be assigned to that destination.	

Table B-2: 1st variant table example for Open a Lane Basic Flow

For the second table the operational variables of Open Gate and Gate Response are the only operational variable listed. The starting System State for each potential test is the ending state of the condition required to begin testing Open Gate values. In this case that state is the same as the expected result of Variant 6 in the first table. I identified that state as "Lane has been assigned, gate not opened ".

Here is the second variant table.

Variant	Sys State	Open Gate	Gate Response	Expected Results	Comments
20	Lane has been assigned, gate not opened	Valid	N/A	The system responds by sending a request to the divert lane control system to open the gate.	
21	Lane has been assigned, gate not opened	Invalid format	N/A	System prompts for valid format	
22	Lane has been assigned, gate not opened	Wrong gate specified	N/A	System indicated the gate cannot be opened and prompts for a different gate.	
23	Lane has been assigned, gate not opened	No Command	N/A	The system waits for an open command	
24	Lane has been assigned, gate not opened	Valid	Gate Open	The system: Stores the gate and destination information Sends the Dispatch System with the lane and destination assignment information indicating packages can be assigned to the lane. Notifies the Conveyor Operator	
25	Lane has been assigned, gate not opened	Valid	Gate Locked Error	The system informs the operator the gate could not be opened	
26	Lane has been assigned, gate not opened	Valid	No response	After ten seconds the system determines the gate can't be opened and informs the operator	
27	Lane has been assigned, gate not opened Selected gate already opened	Valid	N/A	The system informs the Conveyor Operator that the selected gate is already open	
28	No Communication with Dispatch system	Valid	Gate Open	Not sure what the response is	No requirement

Table B3: 2nd variant table example for Open a Lane Basic Flow

Example of a Test Procedure For a Manual GUI Test

Test Procedures for Open a Lane Basic flow Positive Test

Test Procedure 1

Procedure Specific Files

System Output log file: This file contains a log of activity including messages sent, messages received, and information stored during system operation. This file is automatically initialized when the Conveyor Control application is run. No set up is required. File name is SystemLogFile.txt

Dispatch System Output log file: This file contains a log of messages received from the system under test. This file is automatically initialized when the application Dispatch Application is run. No set up is required. File name is DispatchLogFile.txt.

Conveyor Simulator log file: This file contains a log of activities including messages received and sent. This file is automatically initialized when the application Conveyor Simulator Application is run. No set up is required. File name is ConveyorSimulatorLogFile.txt.

Conveyor Simulator parameter table: This file contains parameters to simulate an active conveyor system. It holds information that describes lane assignments the simulated system will be initialized to and the packages that will be simulated as moving through the simulated conveyor system.

File Format: As description of file format can be found in document ConveyorSimulatorParameterFile.doc.

File Parameters: Parameter specifics for this file are described in the document called SimulatorSetUpTP1

File location name: ConveyorSetUpTP1

File location: PC2 folder location c:\Simulator

Set Up: prior to testing access PC2 and copy file ConveyorSetUpTP1 from c:\simulatorSetUpFiles to c:\Simulator

Test Environment Set Up

Test environment setup steps are as follows:

- Turn on Monitor for PC1 (labeled)
- Turn on Monitor for PC2
- Turn on power (black button) for the Conveyor Box (labeled "Conveyor System Box").
- Windows system will be displayed in monitor for PC1.
- Windows System will be displayed in monitor for PC2.
- Select Conveyor Simulator Icon on PC2 using the arrows on the keypad labeled (PC2)
- The monitor for PC Two will display message that the conveyor is running
- Select the Dispatch System on PC1 using the arrows on the keypad labeled (PC1)
- The monitor for PC1 will display message indicating the Dispatch System is running.
- the System Under test (SUT) icon on PC1 using the arrows on the keypad labeled (PC1)
- The monitor for PC1 will display message indicating SUT is running. The Window for Conveyor Monitoring is displayed.

Test Procedure Steps

Step#	TEST Step	EXPECTED RESULT	Pass/Fail	Req	Comments
1	At the Conveyor monitoring display select the "Assign Lane" button.	The Assign Lane window is displayed with the prompt for a destination		SRS5	
2	Select the drop down menu for Destination	The Drop Down Menu shows all available destinations (AAX, BAX, CCS, and CCD)		SRS2	
3	Select AAX from the destination Drop down menu	The Lanes assigned to destination AAX are displayed (Lane 1, 3, 6)		SRS2	
4		Available lanes are displayed ($ and 7)		SRS2	
5	Select Lane 7, enter 100 in Max package field, and select the "Assign Lane" button	Lane 7 is assigned to destination AAX. !00 is set to maximum packages limit. (Verify with the system run log)		SRS5, SRS19	
6		Lane assignment of lane 7 to destination AAX is displayed with a button titled "Open Lane"		SRS6	
7	Click on "Open Lane" button	Open Lane command specifying lane 7 is sent to Divert Lane. (Verify with the simulator log report.		SRS6	
8	View that the simulator displays that the "Gate for Lane 7 Opened" message sent to system under test	System receives message and marks gate 7 as OPEN(Verify in system log)		SRS7 SRS8	
9		Gate and destination information is stored (verify in system log)		SRS12	
10		Lane and destination assignment (lane 7 and AAX) is sent to the dispatch system (Verify in dispatch system log file)		SRS13	
11		A message indicating gate for lane 7 has been opened is displayed		SRS7 SRS8	

Test Evaluation Instructions

Display the system log file (file "SystemLogFile.txt". View the file and verify steps 5, 8, and 9 in the table above.

Display the Simulator system log file (file "ConveyorSimulatorLogFile.txt". View the file and verify step 7 in the table above.

Display the Dispatch system log file (file "DispatchSystemLogFile.txt". View the file and verify step 10 in the table above.

Appendix C Templates

A Test Case Template

Test Case Name/Identifier
Description:
This Test Case validates …. <This can be things such as nominal (happy) path of a UC, Negative tests, etc.>
Add info on how the TC starts and what happens at a general level

Objective:
List high level functionality verified or references to requirements>

- Verify the <system> software performs the functionality of the requirements allocated to this Test Case, per <reference>.
- Verify the <system> software performs the functionality of the <reference use case, sequence diagrams, functions, etc.

Test Items/Requirements Addressed:
List items to test by feature and corresponding requirements. Use requirement ID and description.
For each item, consider supplying references to the following test item documentation:

a) Requirements specification;
b) Design specification;
c) Users guide;
d) Operations guide;
e) Installation guide.

Prerequisite Conditions:
List conditions including other test cases that must run, system states, etc. that must be in place for this test case to run.

Test Inputs (Input Specifications)
Specify each input required to execute the test case. Some of the inputs will be specified by value (with tolerances where appropriate), while others, such as constant tables or transaction files, will be specified by name. Identify all appropriate databases, files, terminal messages, memory resident areas, and values passed by the operating system. Specify all required relationships between inputs (e.g., timing).

Expected Test Results (Output Specifications):
Specify all of the outputs and features (e.g., response time) required of the test items. Provide the exact value (with tolerances where appropriate) for each required output or feature.

Criteria for Evaluating Results:
List any details related to result evaluation. Pass/fail.

Environmental needs

Hardware
Specify the characteristics and configurations of the hardware required to execute this test case.

Software
Specify the system and application software required to execute this test case. This may include system software such as operating systems, compilers, simulators, and test tools. In addition, the test item may interact with application software.

Other
Specify any other requirements such as unique facility needs or specially trained personnel.

Special procedural requirements

Describe any special constraints on the test procedures that execute this test case. These constraints may involve special set up, operator intervention, output determination procedures, and special wrap up.

Test Design (Activity Diagrams):

Activity diagrams or other documentation that tells how the test will be performed go here

Intercase dependencies

List the identifiers of test cases that must be executed prior to this test case. Summarize the nature of the dependencies.

Assumptions and Constraints

A Test Procedure Template

Test Procedures for <test case Name>

Test Procedure 1

Procedure Specific Files and Set up

List the files that need to be set up and their formats including specific values for this procedure. These can include configuration files and specific flight data files that may simulate specific situations.

Test Environment Set Up

Test environment setups are described here. Detailed instructions can be kept in other documents and referred to here.

Test Procedure Steps

The table below will list the steps taken to set up and run the tests. It documents manual activities.

Step#	TEST Step	EXPECTED RESULT	Pass/Fl	Req	Comments
1	Procedure Step 1			Requirement covered	
2	Procedure Step 2				
3					
4					

Test Evaluation Instructions

List evaluation instructions here.

Index